YOU CAN'T CATCH ME

Its claws grip the ground just like running shoes

The **CHEETAH** is the fastest land animal over short distances. In 2012, a captive cheetah at Cincinnati Zoo covered 100 metres in 5.95 seconds, clocking a top speed of 97.6 km/h (61 mph). A cheetah's body is designed for speed, with long legs, a flexible spine, claws that grip the ground just like running shoes and a long tail for balance. Its strides are so fast and so long that all four feet are off the ground for more than half the time. When it is running at maximum speed, it is almost flying.

ANIMAL RECORD BREAKERS

100s of Amazing Facts and Spectacular Feats

JAMES FAIR

PUBLISHED BY THE NATURAL HISTORY MUSEUM, LONDON

CONTENTS

OSTRICH

The world's biggest bird may not be able to fly but it sure can run! In one powerful stride **OSTRICHES** can cover up to 5 metres (16 ft), which is about the length of a medium-sized car. They can run steadily at speeds of 60 km/h (37.5 mph) for 30 minutes – at that pace, they would be able to run a marathon in under 42 minutes, nearly three times faster than the human world record!

KILLER WHALE

One of the ocean's top predators, these super-fast whales can swim at speeds of 55.2 km/h (34.5 mph) when pursuing their prey. And they're not called **KILLER WHALES** for nothing. Hunting together in pods they eat anything from fish and squid to walruses and penguins, even sharks and larger whales! And, combined with their speed, they have some pretty brilliant hunting techniques – whacking icefloes with their huge tails to knock the seals lying on top off and into the water, and even ramming their powerful bodies at full speed into large sharks, flipping them over and then holding them underwater until they suffocate!

PRONGHORN ANTELOPE

Everyone knows the land animal considered the fastest on Earth, but very few know the second fastest. Well, now you do – it's the **PRONGHORN ANTELOPE**, a speed merchant that races across the vast open grasslands of North America. It's been clocked at 96 km/h (60 mph), and over 800 metres (½ mile) it would comfortably outpace a cheetah. Scientists think it may have evolved its turbocharged speed to allow it to escape a now extinct species of American cheetah.

GIANTS

AMUR TIGER

Tigers are the largest of the existing cats, and the **AMUR** or **SIBERIAN TIGER** is often considered the biggest of all. A male can weigh up to 250 kg (550 lb) and be 3 metres (10 ft) long, with the longest ever recorded measuring in at 3.3 metres (11 ft). They are only found in Russia's Far East and northern China, where they hunt large herbivores such as elk (also known as moose) and wild boar. A single tiger can eat up to 27 kg (60 lb) in one night.

GREEN ANACONDA

One seriously powerful predator is the **GREEN ANACONDA**! It's the world's heaviest snake, with the largest ever recorded one weighing 227 kg (500 lb), with a length of 8.43 metres (28 ft), and with a girth of 1.11 metres (3 ⅔ ft). It likes to eat large fish, caiman, rodents and wild pigs, and kills its prey with a bone crunching, organ popping squeeze!

CHINESE GIANT SALAMANDER

The world's largest amphibian is the **CHINESE GIANT SALAMANDER**, which can grow to a length of 1.8 metres (6 ft), the height of a fully grown man, and weigh between 25 to 50 kg (55 to 110 lb). They are the top predators in the cool mountain streams in southern China where they live, feeding on invertebrates, frogs and fish. The yin and yang symbol of Chinese philosophy is said to be based on two giant salamanders intertwined.

AFRICAN ELEPHANT

All elephants are big but the **AFRICAN ELEPHANT** is the biggest, bigger than any other land animal. Males can weigh up to 6.8 tonnes (7.5 tons), which is about the same as two safari trucks or 9 to 10 cows! African elephants also have ears larger than any other animal on Earth, and they are shaped like the continent of Africa, which is where they live! Cool, huh?

OF THE LAND

Shorter than the first segment of an average thumb, the **STAR-SUCKER PYGMY OCTOPUS** measures about 2.5 cm (1 in) long and weighs 1 g (a fraction of an ounce), about half the weight of a standard phone SD card. Found in the Indian and Pacific Oceans, it is officially the world's smallest octopus. It inhabits shallow reefs, where it hunts even tinier crustaceans and shellfish.

SMALL BUT PERFECT

BEE HUMMINGBIRD

There are beetles bigger than the **BEE HUMMINGBIRD**, which is just 5.7 cm (2 ¼ in) long from the end of its beak to the tip of its tail and weighs 1.6 g (a fraction of an ounce). The female lays eggs the size of coffee beans – it's incredible to think anything hatches out of them! Found only in Cuba, in the Caribbean, they must defend their favoured flowers, which they rely on for nectar, from hawkmoths and bumblebees.

ASTERINID SEA STAR

It may be the smallest known starfish, but the **ASTERINID SEA STAR** hides a dark secret. With a diameter of just 0.9 cm (3/8 in), these tiny marine invertebrates produce young about 25–30 per cent of their size. Once they can eat, these voracious offspring feed on their brothers and sisters! They're only found in tidal pools off the Eyre Peninsula of South Australia.

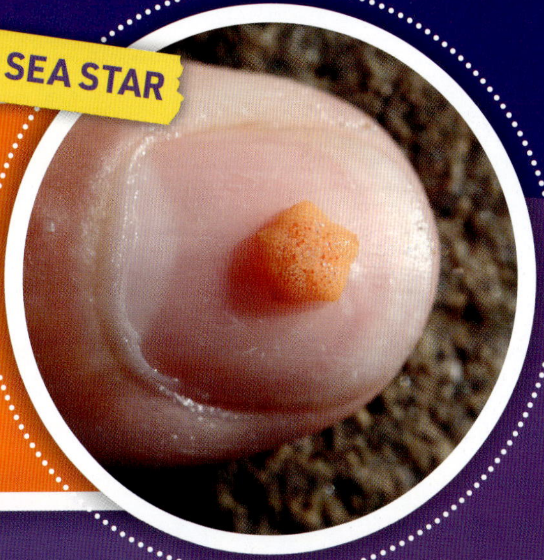

PINK FAIRY ARMADILLO

Looking like they're wearing a quilted eiderdown, **PINK FAIRY ARMADILLOS** are not just strange beasts, they are also the smallest of the group of animals that includes anteaters, armadillos and sloths – just 13 cm (5 in) long, about half the size of a large brown rat. They use their outsized claws to dig burrows and hunt for ants and other insects in the dry scrublands of Argentina where they live.

DON'T MESS WITH ME

This bird's superman-like vision is at least four times sharper than a human's, which means it can spot prey up to 1.6 km (1 mile) away! When they attack, **BALD EAGLES** can swoop down from the sky (though not vertically) at speeds of up to 161 km/h (100 mph). They mainly eat fish – though their diet varies depending on where in North America they are – and they can pluck fish straight from the water with their talons.

CASSOWARY

Like beasts straight out of *Jurassic Park*, **CASSOWARIES** are giant flightless birds with three sharp claws (like the fearsome dinosaur raptors). The middle claw is 12 cm (4 ¾ in) long, and is said to be capable of severing an arm or slicing open a stomach. Often described as the world's most dangerous birds, the three species of cassowary, which are found in Australia and New Guinea, attack and occasionally kill people they see as a threat.

BURMESE PYTHON

This huge snake is famous for the way it catches and eats its food. It uses its fangs to grab hold of its prey, then coils its body around it, squeezing tighter and tighter until the animal suffocates, and then swallows it whole. Stretchy ligaments in its jaws allow it to swallow animals much wider than its head. One **BURMESE PYTHON** living in the Everglades National Park, USA (pythons are not native to the USA, they were introduced there by people getting rid of unwanted pets), even tried to swallow an alligator – it turned out to be too big and the snake exploded!

ANT ASSASSIN BUG

The **ANT ASSASSIN BUG** lies in wait on ant trails, oozing a chemical that ants find irresistible. Once an ant is close enough the assassin bug stabs it in the back of the head, then injects a venom into the ant that paralyzes it in a matter of seconds. After sucking the juices out of its victim, the bug wears the empty ant body on its own back as camouflage, to confuse its predators. It can carry as many as 20 dead ants at a time.

ATTACK AT YOUR PERIL!

BLUE DRAGON

Though just 3 cm (1.2 in) long, the **BLUE DRAGON** packs a remarkable punch. A species of sea slug or nudibranch, it spends its days floating through the water, often upside down, feeding on its preferred prey of Portuguese man o' wars. It keeps the man o' wars' stinging nematocysts and stores them in its finger-like cerata so it can deliver a potent sting of its own if touched by another animal. Sneaky.

BOXER CRAB

With a tentacled sea anemone in each claw, a **BOXER CRAB** does indeed look like it's wearing a bizarre pair of boxing gloves. And while they use the anemones to defend themselves, the crabs also steal food from them, a way of feeding known as kleptoparasitism. They are also sometimes called pom-pom crabs because the anemones make them look like cheerleaders. And they deliberately starve the anemones to keep them small.

MANTIS SHRIMP

MANTIS SHRIMPS are medium-sized, often exotically coloured crustaceans of the marine world, renowned for their specially adapted forelimbs, which they use for hunting. There are more than 400 species spread around the world, and they are split into two distinct groups – smashers, which club their prey, and spearers, which pierce them. Peacock mantis shrimps strike so fast that they create shock waves, which help kill their prey.

MALAYSIAN EXPLODING ANT

Making yourself explode might sound like a poor defensive strategy, but it works for the **MALAYSIAN EXPLODING ANT**. When attacked by a predator, the ant explodes, coating its assailant in an adhesive toxic secretion that can even cause death. The ant might have killed itself, but it has potentially saved the rest of its colony – the ultimate self-sacrifice.

PINOCCHIO LIZARD

This weird-looking, very rare lizard has an extra long snout that gives the species its name. The **PINOCCHIO LIZARD**, also referred to as the horned anole, was thought to be extinct but was rediscovered in 2005 in the cloud forests of Ecuador. Only the males have a long nose, and videos taken by scientists appear to show the noses being used as a sign of dominance in display fights as well as during courtship.

UNICORNFISH

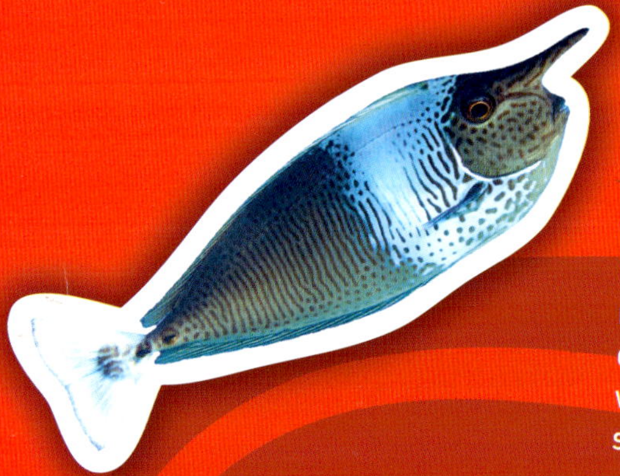

With a single horn growing from the top of its head, the **UNICORNFISH** fully justifies its name. The horn starts to grow in early adulthood, but nobody knows what it's for. It doesn't appear to be for fighting; the fish uses its razor-sharp tail spines for that! Maybe it's used to show off to other unicornfish, or in displays of colour change, which the fish can do almost instantly depending on its surroundings and mood.

HOODED SEAL

Is this the strangest looking seal you ever saw – a seal that blows its nose up like a balloon? Only male **HOODED SEALS** have an enlarged nose, which looks like a black wrinkled hood on top of their heads when it's not inflated. When the males do inflate their hood it can double the size of their head – which is useful if you're trying to scare away potential threats or impress a mate. Another trick hooded seals have is to blow up a bright red skin-membrane balloon from the inside of their left nostril. Lucky there aren't many sharp objects in the Arctic!

LIKE MY NOSE?

PROBOSCIS MONKEY

The super-sized dangling nose of the male **PROBOSCIS MONKEY**, a species found only on the island of Borneo, can be up to 18 cm (7 in) long! It's thought that big noses work like an echo chamber and help amplify the male's calls – a female proboscis monkey then judges the male's attractiveness on how loud the call is. The bigger and stronger the monkey, the more exaggerated his nose is.

How weird is this?!

NATURAL DISGUISE

ORCHID MANTIS

When your whole body is as beautiful as the flowers around, you don't need any camouflage – that's the evolutionary strategy of the **ORCHID MANTIS**, whose colouration disguises it as a flower to attract passing insects, which it can then kill and eat. Orchid mantises, which are found in Southeast Asia, take a range of prey including crickets, bees, flies and butterflies. Like most mantis species, females are larger than the males and can reach 10 cm (4 in) long.

Good luck spotting a **LEAF-MIMICKING KATYDID** hiding among the leaves. Their whole bodies are flattened into the shape of a leaf, even displaying a central leaf rib. No two insects are alike – some look like new green leaves whereas others appear brown, speckled or decaying, with fake holes made of see-through skin. Some also sway in the wind to mimic the movement of leaves blowing in a breeze.

LEAF-MIMICKING KATYDID

SPHINX MOTH CATERPILLAR

Is that a slithering snake? No, it's the **SPHINX MOTH CATERPILLAR** and one of the best mimics in nature. When threatened by a swooping bird or pouncing lizard, the caterpillar dangles from a twig, twists its head round and inflates the end of its body into a diamond shape, revealing two large snake eyes. If the attacker isn't fooled by the clever disguise, the caterpillar lunges towards it in a snake-like strike.

LEAF-TAILED GECKOS are found in both Australia and Madagascar, though the two groups of animals are not related (other than both being geckos). So they are great examples of convergent evolution – where two different animals separately develop similar features. The broken patterns on their body, resembling lichen on trees or rocks, and their flattened leaf-shaped tails, make them almost invisible in their rainforest habitat – which is ideal for the sit-and-wait predators they are.

LEAF-TAILED GECKO

FOUR-HORNED ANTELOPE

Most animals that have horns or tusks are happy with just a pair, but the **FOUR-HORNED ANTELOPE** – as its name implies – has evolved to have four in total, though the front pair are often little more than 2.5 cm (1 in) long. Four-horned antelopes are mainly found in India (with a few in Nepal) where they live in areas of dry forests and grasslands. They are rare and shy and so not often seen.

Introducing the **MARKHOR** – the goat with horns that look as if they could be used to drill through solid rock! The male's horns can grow to 160 cm (63 in), the height of a teenage boy. The markhor's stronghold is the Karakoram mountains of India and Pakistan, and it is renowned for its ability to scale steep cliffs. It is also one of the key animals that snow leopards prey on.

MARKHOR

ACTUAL SIZE
1 metre/
3 ft 3 in

WILD WATER BUFFALO

The horns of a **WILD WATER BUFFALO** grow in a massive symmetrical arc, and one bull is recorded as having horns measuring 4.24 metres (14 ft) from one tip to the other (following the horns' curve), though 1 metre (3 ft 3 in) is more common. The wild water buffalo – the ancestor of the domesticated version, which has a global population of nearly 200 million animals – is also the world's heaviest bovid and is now only found in India, Nepal, Bhutan and Thailand.

Who said the dinosaurs died out? Triceratops is alive and well and inhabiting mountain forests in southern Kenya and northern Tanzania, though in a much reduced size. Of course, **THREE-HORNED CHAMELEONS** aren't related to the dinosaurs, but they are strikingly reminiscent. Up to 35 cm (13 ¾ in) long, the species is also found in the US states of California, Florida and Hawaii, where they have been introduced.

THREE-HORNED CHAMELEON

HOW MANY HORNS?

WHAT'S FOR DINNER?

DUNG BEETLE

Many invertebrates survive on a diet of poo, but only **DUNG BEETLES** have turned this into an art form. There are different lifestyles among the 5,000 or so species, but perhaps the most sophisticated are those where males roll some dung into a huge ball (often considerably larger than they are) and offer it to the females as a sort of present. Females can lay their eggs in the ball, which then provides nutrition for their larvae.

EWWW!

MANED WOLF

Members of the dog family are mostly hunters and meat-eaters, but the **MANED WOLVES** of South America's grasslands are different, and not just because of their long, stilt-like legs. About half their diet consists of fruit and other plant matter, and they are especially keen on the small tomato-like fruits of the lobeira plant. Indeed, the plant gets its common name – 'fruta do lobo', which translates as fruit of the wolf – as a result of this.

COMMON SHREW

It doesn't sound much fun being a shrew. Because of their tiny size, **COMMON SHREWS** lose their body heat so quickly that they are said to be always two or three hours from death. They must therefore forage on an almost constant basis for insects and other invertebrates and eat 90 per cent of their body weight (a maximum of 14 g (½ oz)) every day.

HOUSE CENTIPEDE

HOUSE CENTIPEDES are like walking shopping trolleys. They scurry around on their 15 pairs of legs and, when they kill a tasty morsel such as a fly or silverfish, they can hold it in one of their pairs of legs instead of eating it straight away. They have the ability to carry multiple prey items in this way if they wish. Originally native to southern Europe and North Africa, they are now also found in North America and northern Europe.

SPECIAL POWERS

LILY TROTTERS, or jacanas, are birds that are just one step away from being able to walk on water, which is why they are sometimes also referred to as Jesus birds. There are eight species spread across Africa, Asia, Australia and South America, and they all have extra-long toes giving them a massive toe span – up to 15 cm (6 in). The toes spread their weight as they move around freely on lily pads and other floating vegetation.

RACCOON DOG

The only members of the dog family to hibernate, and looking – as their name suggests – more like a raccoon, **RACCOON DOGS** are native to Southeast and East Asia. In some parts of the world they are farmed for their fur, and this has helped them spread into Europe, as has their remarkable adaptability. They have a wide-ranging diet that includes small mammals and birds, invertebrates, fruits and, well really, any dead animals.

HERRMANN'S SEA CUCUMBER

Resembling a giant gherkin, **HERRMANN'S SEA CUCUMBER** (referred to in some parts of where it lives as the curryfish) can grow to 1 metre (40 in) long, with a diameter of 24 cm (10 in). Ranging in colour from bright green to yellow-gold and brown, this fantastic beast contains compounds, such as glycosides, carotenoids and peptides, that accelerate the healing of wounds. It's found over a wide area of the Indian and western Pacific Oceans.

JAGUARUNDI

The head is slightly strange though unmistakably feline, but the long and sinuous neck and body of the **JAGUARUNDI** is something else completely and reminiscent of an otter or American marten. That's not all that's strange about this medium-sized cat, which is found from southern USA to Argentina. Like a cheetah, it cannot fully retract the claws on its hind paws, and the sounds it makes range from purring and whistling to chirping like a bird.

NOW YOU SEE 'EM,

PEPPERED MOTH

This animal's not wearing an invisibility cloak, it's just really good at blending in. The light speckled colouring of the **PEPPERED MOTH** perfectly matches the lichen-covered trees and rocks it likes to rest on, making it hard to see. It also provides a great example of evolution in action. In Britain, when pollution was high during the industrial revolution and buildings and trees were covered in soot, a darker form of the peppered moth became the dominant one as it was harder to see.

FLOWER CRAB SPIDER

Most spiders spin webs to trap insects, but not **FLOWER CRAB SPIDERS**. Instead they ambush their prey and deliver a paralyzing bite. They feed on pollinators attracted to flowers, such as bees, flies and butterflies, but to do this they need to be invisible. Luckily the females can change colour to match their chosen flower. And, they also run sideways like a crab.

NOW YOU DON'T

CUTTLEFISH

This sea creature is a master of disguise. The **CUTTLEFISH**, which isn't actually a fish but an intelligent invertebrate related to the octopus, can quickly change its skin colour. And for an animal that's probably colourblind that's pretty amazing! Its skin is covered in thousands of colour-changing cells, which can contract to create a shade to match its surroundings. It can even flash moving colour patterns along its body to communicate with other cuttlefish.

THORNY DEVIL

These lizards are found in Australia and resemble the ancient reptiles of the dinosaur era. Their camouflaging shades of desert brown and tan make **THORNY DEVILS** hard to spot, and they move in a bizarre rocking manner which, it's thought, may confuse any potential predators. Thorny devils even change the tones of their skin to match the weather conditions – they are paler when it's warmer and darker when it's cooler. Covered from head to toe in sharp spines, and with a false head on the back of their neck, they aren't easy to swallow either.

WHEN THE GOING GETS TOUGH

CAMEL

Even in very hot, dry conditions, **CAMELS** can go a week without drinking any water, and several months at other times. They can do this thanks to their distinctive hump, a feature that stores not water but fat, which can be broken down in times of need to produce energy and water. A camel's hump gets bigger or smaller depending on how well-fed the camel is, and can contain 50 kg (110 lb) of fat in an animal weighing 500 kg (1,100 lb).

A camel's hump can get bigger or smaller

ARCTIC FOX

Weighing just an average of 3.5 kg (7 ¾ lb), less than most domestic cats, **ARCTIC FOXES** are small but perfectly adapted for life in the polar north. A white coat several inches thick in winter (becoming grey-brown or blue-grey in summer) means they can survive in a temperature of -70°C (-94°F), and they even have fur on the pads on their feet to reduce heat loss. They produce more pups than you might expect, averaging 11 in a litter.

MUDSKIPPER

A fish out of water is an expression meaning something that's out of place – but that's not true of **MUDSKIPPERS**, which have evolved to be very comfortable on dry land. They can do this by storing water in their large gill chambers, as well as absorbing oxygen from the air through their skin. They come out of the water to feed on crustaceans and other small animals and are found in swamps and estuaries from Africa to Polynesia.

KANGAROO RAT

Even camels have to drink water, but the **KANGAROO RATS** of North America's desert habitats have evolved to never need a drop. Instead they eat dry seeds from which they can extract water – they can extract half a gram of water out of every gram of seeds they consume – and their kidneys help conserve water by concentrating their urine to an almost crystal-like consistency. They have powerful back legs which allow them to leap 2.7 metres (9 ft) in a single bound.

SLOWLY DOES IT

The tortoise beat the hare in the fabled race but, on the whole, these ancient reptiles are not known for being fast movers. The **MOJAVE DESERT TORTOISE**, which is only found in California's Mojave Desert, has had its speed measured at 3 to 8 metres (10 to 26 ft) a minute, which is equivalent to a maximum speed of 0.5 km/h (0.3 mph).

Even though **SEA ANEMONES** take their name from a flower, they are animals and can move around, albeit very slowly. Researchers have used time-lapse photography to measure their speed at about 1 cm (0.4 in) an hour. Normally they are attached to rocks by a single sticky foot, but if they need to move away quickly they let go of the rock and float freely in the water currents.

SEA ANEMONE

It is very hard to measure the speed of animals that move very slowly, but one study found that **GARDEN SNAILS** travel up to 25 metres (82 ½ ft) in a 24-hour period, equivalent to 0.001 km/h (0.0006 mph), making ponderous plodders such as tortoises look quite speedy. Snails move by sliding over the ground on their singular muscular foot. As they crawl along they lubricate the ground with a slimy mucus secreted from their foot. Slippery!

GARDEN SNAIL

YELLOW BANANA SLUG

YELLOW BANANA SLUGS are huge, yellow and very, very slow, moving at a maximum speed of 16.5 cm (6 ½ in) a minute, equivalent to about 10 metres (33 ft) an hour or 0.01 km/h (0.006 mph). They can grow to a length of 18 to 23 cm (7 to 9 in), making them the second largest slug in the world. They eat rotting organic matter, but also fruits such as blackberries and raspberries.

FEATHERTAIL GLIDER

There are a number of marsupials that have evolved the ability to glide, but the **FEATHERTAIL GLIDER** – which weighs an average of just 12 g (2/5 oz), or the equivalent of three teaspoons of sugar – also has remarkable, serrated toe pads. These allow it to cling to smooth surfaces, including a vertical pane of glass. This mouse-sized acrobat can be found in woodlands in eastern and southern Australia.

HYRAX

Having elephants and manatees as your closest relatives suggests that you're not going to be especially skilled at climbing. But that's not the case with **HYRAXES** – rotund little mammals about the size of a small dog that are found in Africa and the Middle East. Though they have hoof-like nails, the soles of their feet are rubbery and, when they climb trees or rocks, this creates a suction effect, helping them to stick to the surface.

ROCKY MOUNTAIN GOAT

Someone who's very sure-footed in rough and steep terrain is often described as a mountain goat – and with good reason. The **ROCKY MOUNTAIN GOAT** of North America can scale slopes as steep as 60° thanks to hooves with rubber-like soles to aid grip and strong neck and shoulder muscles. These provide the goat with the power to propel itself almost vertically upwards.

EXTRA GRIP

GECKOS make up one-quarter of all known lizard species (nearly 1,500 geckos out of 6,000 in total), and 60 per cent of them have a unique system of microscopic hairs, known as setae, on their toepads. These setae provide them with extraordinary adhesive powers, enabling them to cling to and scale vertical and even inverted surfaces. Scientists have studied the properties of the setae and how they aid adhesion to develop biologically inspired technologies.

MOVERS

BLUE-FOOTED BOOBY

BLUE-FOOTED BOOBIES gained their common name from Spanish explorers, who saw their rather comical courtship dance and their lack of fear of humans and called them 'bobo', which means silly or foolish. The dance involves the males repeatedly placing their feet quite slowly and deliberately on the ground and occasionally bowing their heads or looking directly upwards until the females join in.

EUROPEAN YELLOW-TAILED SCORPION

Males of several species of scorpion, including the EUROPEAN YELLOW-TAILED SCORPION, lead females on a courtship dance in which the male holds the female by her claws, or pedipalps. During this dance, males sometimes appear to sting their partners, but scientists don't know if they actually inject venom or why they do it. One theory is that the injection of a weaker 'pre-venom' calms the female.

AND SHAKERS

DUSKY DOLPHIN

There are so many cetaceans that perform amazing stunts it would be hard to award a prize for the most acrobatic, but the DUSKY DOLPHIN would certainly be one of the contenders. It's said that duskies can perform 36 breaches, or full leaps out of the water, in one bout, and that in any large group, there is always at least one in mid-air. They are relatively small dolphins found in temperate waters of the southern hemisphere.

SNOW LEOPARD

A SNOW LEOPARD was once observed leaping a ditch 15 metres (49 ft) wide, a distance roughly the same as the length of an articulated lorry, and eight times the length of its own body. The species' remarkable agility enables it to hunt wild goats such as ibex and markhor in rugged, rocky mountainous areas of Central Asia where it lives.

SUPER-SIZE EARS

ANTELOPE JACKRABBIT

The jackrabbits of North America were given their name by early settlers because of their outsized ears. 'Jackass' – or donkey – rabbits, they called them, and that was eventually shortened to jackrabbit. The **ANTELOPE JACKRABBIT** has the longest ears of any hare or rabbit – up to 17.3 cm (6⅘ in) from head to tip. They're not just good for hearing – blood vessels in the ears help them lose excess body heat during hot weather.

LONG-EARED JERBOA

This tiny rodent looks like a mixture of several different animals. It has a mouse-like body, rabbity ears and a kangaroo-like hop! The **LONG-EARED JERBOA** has the longest ears on the planet compared with its head-body size, which ranges between 7 and 9 cm (2 ¾ and 3 ½ in). Its ears can be half that long. They help to cool the jerboa in hot desert temperatures, and they can hear predators from very far away. It relies on its amazing jumping abilities to dodge danger when it's out foraging by quickly hopping sideways or up to 1.8 metres (6 ft) in the air.

SPOTTED BAT

Meet the bat with ears more than half the length of its body. The **SPOTTED BAT**, which is found from northern Mexico to southern Canada, has a maximum body length of up to 7 cm (2 ¾ in), and its ears are a whopping 4 cm (1 ½ in) long. Like most of their relatives, spotted bats use their ears for echolocation, but their disproportionate size has another function – detecting the low-frequency rustling sounds of their prey.

FENNEC FOX

These petite desert-dwellers of North Africa and the Middle East are the smallest and the cutest of the world's foxes, but with the largest ears! At 10 to 15 cm (4 to 6 in) long they look a bit over-sized, especially given that their head-body length is only about 36 to 41 cm (14 to 16 in). Their ears aren't just for show – they keep the **FENNEC FOXES** cool in their hot home by releasing body heat and help them listen for small prey hiding underground.

LONGEST TONGUES

OKAPI

The **OKAPI**, also known as the forest or zebra giraffe, has one of the longest and most mobile tongues in the animal kingdom. Estimated at between 36 and 46 cm (14 and 18 in) in length., it is so long that an okapi can easily reach up to lick and clean its own eyes. And it is an extraordinary livid purple-black in colour!

GIANT ANTEATER

The tongue of the **GIANT ANTEATER** can be pushed out a remarkable 61 cm (24 in) beyond the tip of its snout – and, incredibly, up to 160 times a minute! The tongue is covered with hundreds of little hooks, which allow the anteater to capture and gobble up 30,000–35,000 ants and termites a day.

CHAMELEON

All lizards have extendable tongues, but the longest by far belongs to the **CHAMELEON**! A chameleon's tongue can be catapulted forward and stretched to a length as long as its own body and, in some species, up to one and half times its body length. A sticky mucus on the end of the tongue helps the chameleon catch its prey. The tongue is so strong that it can pull in about half the chameleon's own body weight.

SUN BEAR

At around 1.2–1.5 metres (4–5 ft) long, **SUN BEARS** are the tiniest bears in the world. They love honey so much that they climb great heights to find it. Their large claws help them cling onto the tree trunks while they use their 20–25 cm (8–10 in) super long tongues to lick honey out of bees' nests. Luckily they aren't bothered by bee stings!

WHAT A

HOWLER MONKEY

With the ability to make a call that can be heard up to nearly 5 km (3 miles) away in the right conditions, **HOWLER MONKEYS**, which are found in Central and South America, may be the loudest terrestrial mammal on Earth. The call, which sounds more like a bark or a roar than a howl, is used by howler monkey groups to let other groups know where they are and to stake their claim to particular feeding trees.

CRACKER BUTTERFLY

There are about 20 butterfly species in the *Hamadryas* genus, otherwise known as **CRACKER BUTTERFLIES**. They are found from Arizona to South America, and all have a most unbutterfly-like ability – they make clicking or cracking noises by clapping their wings together. They do this as a warning when they are approached by potential predators, to defend their territories from other butterflies and (in at least one species) during courtship.

AMERICAN ALLIGATOR

Male **AMERICAN ALLIGATORS** make low-pitched rumbling roars, or bellows, which they use to size each other up when competing for females. These roars allow males to compete with each other without actually fighting and risking potentially lethal injuries, and help females pick a mate. The males' bellows are also accompanied by a unique 'water dance' in which water droplets sprinkle over their backs.

RACKET

NEW GUINEA SINGING DOG

NEW GUINEA SINGING DOGS do not literally sing, but they do make very unusual noises that are unlike any other member of the dog family. They howl in chorus at the start and the end of the day, making a haunting, shriek-like call. Experts differ in their opinion as to whether the dogs are a separate species, or whether they are domestic dogs that have reverted to the wild. And there is much we don't understand about their origins or how they arrived in New Guinea.

SWORD-BILLED HUMMINGBIRDS have a bill longer than their body and the longest bill of any hummingbird. Their bills can measure up to 12 cm (4 ¾ in), which is longer than the palm of an average human hand. Found in mountainous regions of South America, their long bills mean that they can feed on nectar in plants with very deep flowers that other birds cannot reach. Their bills are so long that they cannot use them to preen themselves, so they use their feet instead.

SWORD-BILLED HUMMINGBIRD

YELLOW-BELLIED SAPSUCKER

Woodpeckers drum on tree trunks with their beaks to mark their territories, attract a mate and to search for food. They can strike at a speed of 6 to 7 metres (20 to 23 ft) per second, and one species, the **YELLOW-BELLIED SAPSUCKER**, can deliver 100 to 300 blows in a minute. How they do this without knocking themselves unconscious is down to special adaptations such as a spongy bone between their head and their beak, and the unique way in which the beak itself is constructed.

BRILLIANT

HORNBILL

With their huge, colourful beaks, **HORNBILLS** superficially resemble toucans, though the two groups of birds are not closely related. There is one big difference in appearance, however – hornbills also have a feature known as a casque above their beak. Casques are hollow and they amplify the hornbills' calls, helping them to carry further in the forests of Asia where they live (though they are also found in sub-Saharan Africa).

BEAKS

TOUCAN beaks aren't just crazily coloured and colossal in relation to the rest of their bodies. They are also brilliant examples of lightweight strength. They are made up of tiles, which have outer layers of keratin (the same substance that forms hair and fingernails) with a 'foam' of bony fibres and drum-like membranes sandwiched in the middle. 'It's almost as if the toucan has a deep knowledge of mechanical engineering,' remarked one scientist who investigated the beak's properties.

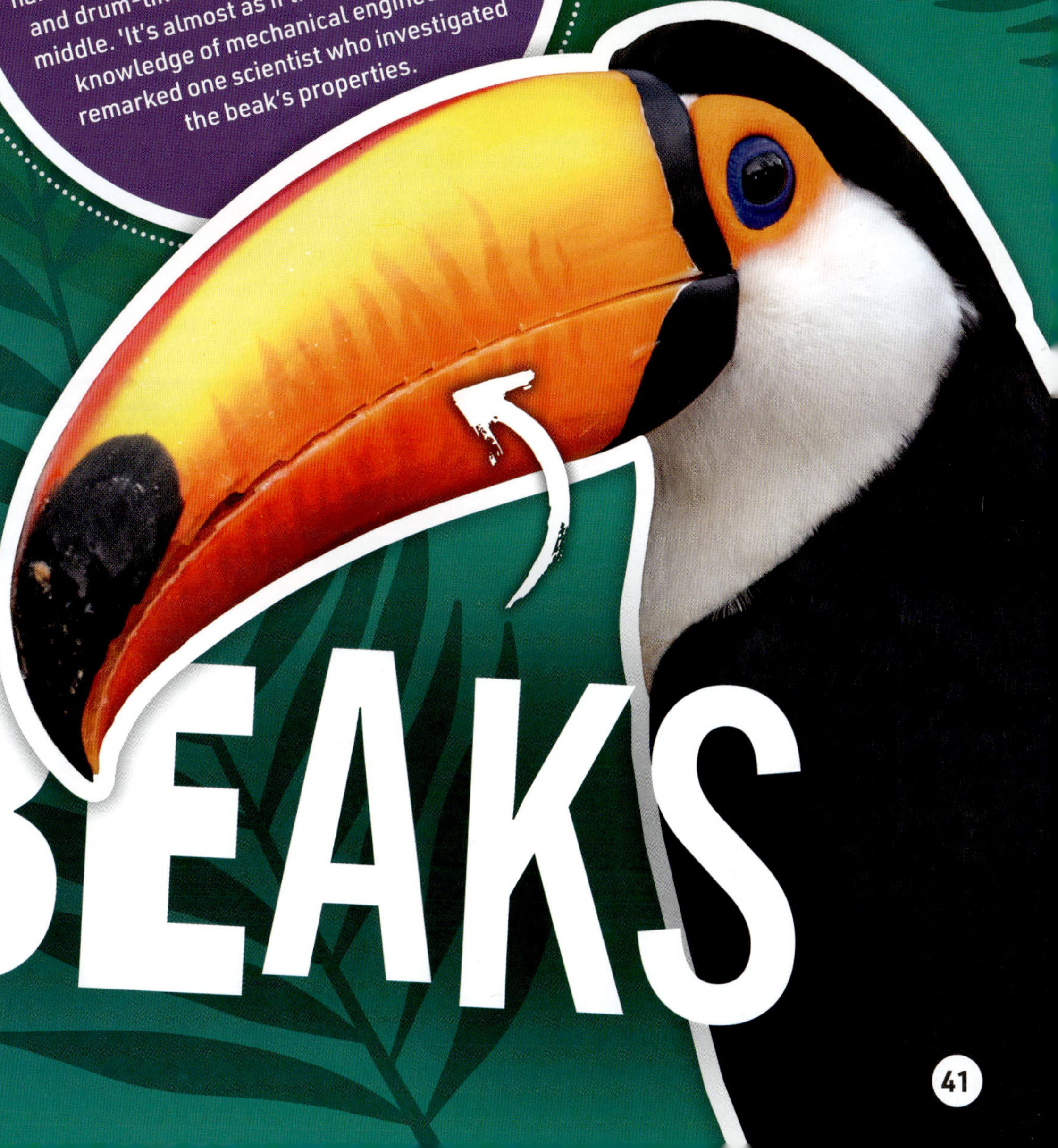

JUMPING SPIDER

Found all over the world, **JUMPING SPIDERS** are a large family with an estimated 6,000 species, and they have four pairs of eyes and excellent vision. The biggest, forward-facing eyes detect colour and fine detail and, though they have a narrow field of view, they can be moved like searchlights. The secondary sets of eyes are less sensitive but have an excellent field of vision, and they help the spiders direct their principal eyes to a potential victim or threat.

FOUR-EYED FISH

What! Four eyes? When it comes to the three species in the genus *Anableps*, **FOUR-EYED FISH** really do have four eyes. Their eyes have separate corneas and pupils and, though only a single lens, it is shaped differently in the different sections. They hunt in inter-tidal zones and use their eyes above the water's surface to look for terrestrial insects and small crabs, while those below enable them to see under the surface too.

EURASIAN WOODCOCK

Most birds have eyes on the sides of their heads, giving them great all-round vision, but woodcocks top them all by also having their eyes set very high and very far back. The **EURASIAN WOODCOCK** is one of eight species worldwide. It is reasonably common across northern Europe and Asia, but it is secretive and elusive, and its 360° vision means it always sees you before you see it.

SUPER SIGHT

CHAMELEON

With eyes that look as if they could rotate like spinning discs, large mouths and brightly coloured skin, **CHAMELEONS** have a cartoonish appearance. But there's nothing funny about their vision. Their eyes operate independently of each other, so one can look out behind for danger while the other is looking forwards for prey such as insects. They also have excellent colour vision – the density of cone cells, which are the cells that detect colour, is similar to that in humans and birds of prey.

WHAT A PONG!

GORILLA

Adult male **GORILLAS**, known as silverbacks, can release a strong odour from their armpits – a bit like many adult humans really. The difference is that gorillas use it as a signal of excitement or aggression and to warn other members of their group of impending danger. In one study of Western lowland gorillas, the odour coming from a silverback was strongest when they were angry, distressed or when they were separated from the mother of their youngest infant.

SPOTTED SKUNK

No, it's not the annual animal gymnastics competition; **SPOTTED SKUNKS** stand on their hands as a warning to predators that they are about to dish out a foul-smelling spray. They are tiny cousins of the more common striped skunks, weighing just 0.9 kg (2.2 lb) or the same as a bag of sugar. Like their relatives, spotted skunks are found throughout North America, though they are elusive and only live in remote areas.

AMERICAN OPOSSUM

The only marsupial found in North America, the **AMERICAN** or **VIRGINIA OPOSSUM** has a neat trick up its furry sleeve for dealing with predators. When in the presence of danger, it goes into a comatose state that fools the other animal into thinking it's not worth eating. American opossums can also release a foul-smelling, greenish-coloured anal fluid and drool from their mouth and nose to make the predator think they are sick.

The **HOATZIN** or **STINK BIRD**, is the bird equivalent of a cow. It feeds on leaves and has evolved special fermentation chambers, much like a cow's multiple stomachs, to break down the tough leaf cellulose. During the digestion process, it gives off methane which makes it smell strongly of manure. Native to the Amazon Basin, it's weird in other ways too – both in how it looks and the fact that its young hatch with claws sprouting from forelimbs.

HOATZIN

WATCH OUT FOR

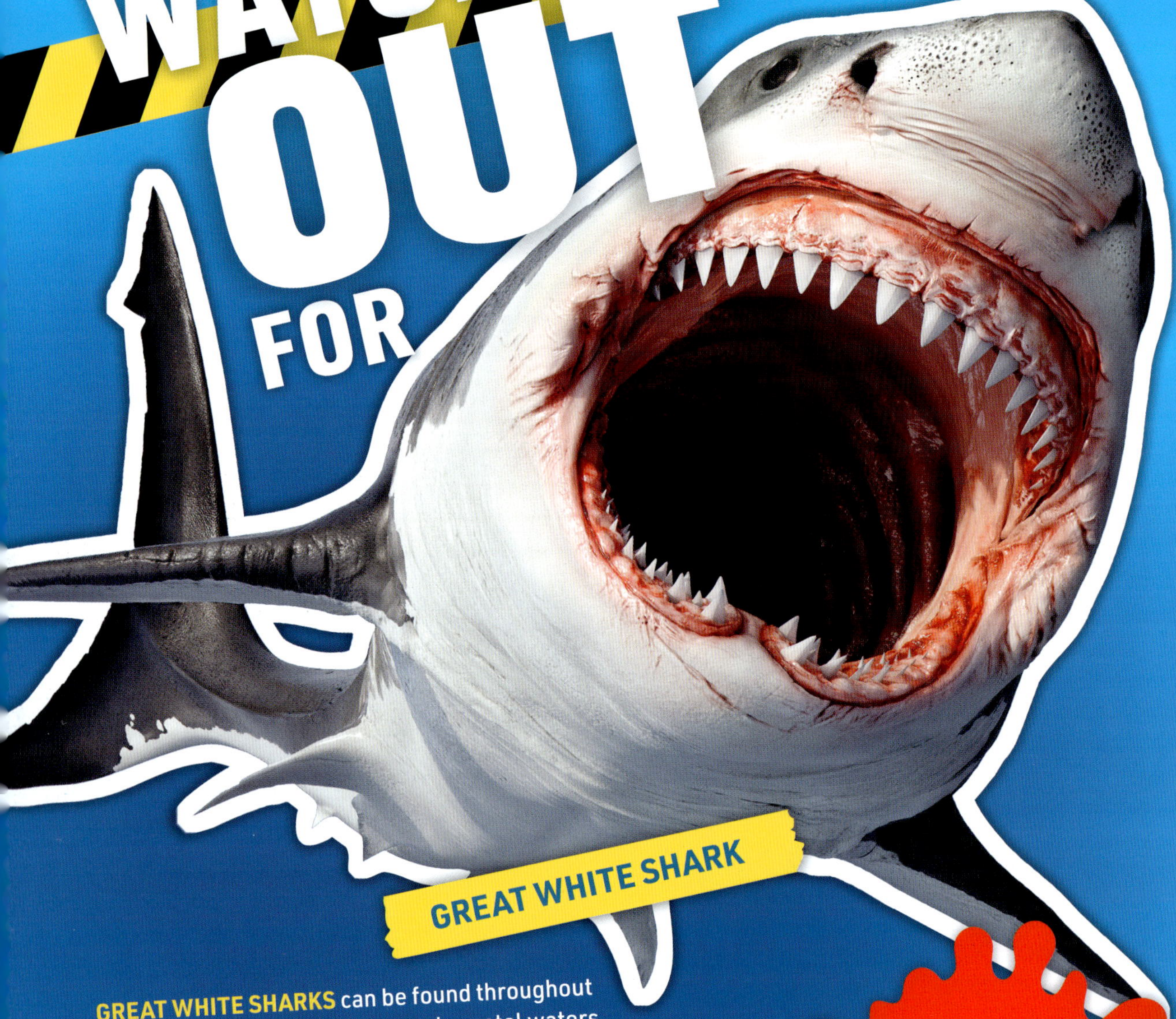

GREAT WHITE SHARK

GREAT WHITE SHARKS can be found throughout the world's oceans, mostly in cool coastal waters. They average around 4.5 metres (14 ¾ ft) long, but some have been measured at a whopping 6 metres (20 ft). These super swimmers have massive jaws full of razor-sharp teeth. They like to take their prey by surprise in sneak attacks, usually swimming up from underneath and snapping up their meal as they leap out of the water.

Their mouths are lined with 300 serrated, triangular teeth in up to seven rows!

POLAR BEAR

POLAR BEARS are the largest land carnivores (meat eaters) in the world, and they are seriously big! A male adult polar bear can grow to 3 metres (10 ¾ ft) long and the heaviest animals weigh as much as ten men. Though potentially one of the most dangerous predators on the planet, attacks on humans are very rare. They have an incredible sense of smell which they use to sniff out their prey up to a kilometre (⅝ mile) away and can even smell seals under the thick Arctic ice.

BLUE-RINGED OCTOPUS

The most dangerous octopuses are the **BLUE-RINGED OCTOPUSES.** The bite of these deceptively pretty creatures can kill in a matter of minutes although, strangely, some people are only mildly affected. They are small animals, just 10–20 cm (4–8 in) across, and they normally attack only when they are taken out of the water and provoked.

TWO-STRIPED WALKINGSTICK

Although most stick insects are harmless creatures, some hiss alarmingly, others attempt to slash predators with their sharp-spurred hind legs, and a few can bite. One of the most dangerous is probably the **TWO-STRIPED WALKINGSTICK** from the southern USA. It is able to squirt a milky spray over a distance of up to 40 cm (15 ¾ in) that can cause temporary blindness in humans.

AS QUICK AS A FLASH

WHITE-HANDED GIBBON

Among the fastest of all apes is the **WHITE-HANDED GIBBON**. It is so fast that, when swinging among the trees, it barely touches a branch before swinging off and grabbing the next. In this way, gibbons can reach speeds of 56 km/h (35 mph) and can still change direction in a split second. They have extraordinarily long arms, one and a half times the length of their legs – a siamang (the largest gibbon species) has an arm span of 1.5 metres (5 ft), and they are only 90 cm (3 ft) tall!

SOUTHERN GIANT DARNER

Dragonflies are the fighter jets of the insect world, and the **SOUTHERN GIANT DARNER** of eastern Australia may be the fastest! Observations dating back to 1917 clocked it at 96 km/h (60 mph). The maximum recorded speed is closer to 58 km/h (36 mph), but it could still comfortably outpace the fastest human over 100 metres (328 ft) – humans can achieve a pace of 36 km/h (22.5 mph) over that distance. Dragonflies can also hover in mid-air and even fly backwards.

CAT FLEA

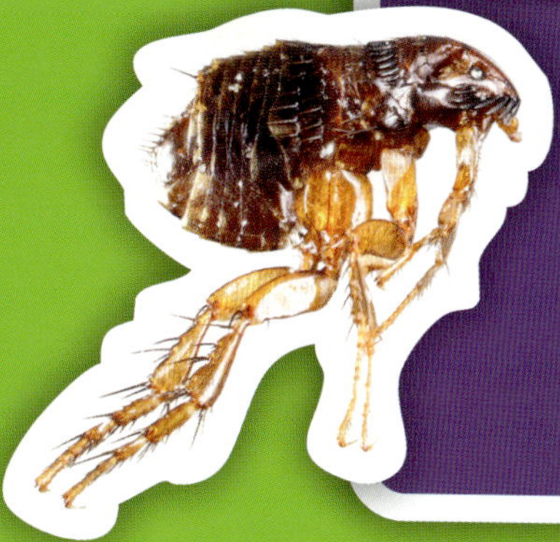

The **CAT FLEA** jumps with an acceleration equivalent to over 20 times that needed to launch a space rocket! Its springy leap is all down to the power stored in a pad of rubber-like material called resilin at the top of its back legs. And it can jump up to 34 cm (13 in). Many fleas are capable of jumping nonstop for many hours, or even several days, without a rest.

TRAP-JAW ANT

Mind your fingers! A **TRAP-JAW ANT** can close its mandibles (jaws) at lightning speed – nearly 800 times faster than a human can blink. And what's also amazing is that they can use their jaws to launch themselves off the ground and up into the air. To confuse predators that want to eat them, groups of ants start jumping all at once, like popcorn popping, making it harder to grab just one.

BOMBARDIER BEETLE

When the **BOMBARDIER BEETLE** feels threatened, it cooks up a boiling, noxious chemical mixture in its abdomen, then squirts it out from its anus with an explosive force, accompanied by an audible 'pfut' sound. That's quite a fart – not silent, but still deadly. There are 250 species, found on every continent apart from Antarctica. One study found toads that swallowed a bombardier beetle regurgitated them back up alive nearly 50 per cent of the time.

HORNED LIZARD

Spitting cobras fire venom at their prey and archerfish knock insects over with water droplets, but the most extreme use of bodily fluids is by the **HORNED LIZARD**, which squirts blood from its eyes to deter an attack. They increase the blood pressure in their heads, which builds up until it ruptures the vessels in their eyes. Found in the western USA and Mexico, horned lizards move their eye muscles to control the direction of the stream of blood.

NORTHERN FULMAR

The **NORTHERN FULMAR** might resemble a gull, but it is actually a close relative of the albatross and petrel. And it hides a dark secret – the ability to spit out a foul-smelling, sticky oil that, it's said, is impossible to wash out of your clothes, or for a bird to preen out of its feathers. Beware if you get too close! This stinky habit is where the fulmar gets its name – it means 'foul bird' in old Norse.

UNEXPECTED DEFENCES

SPERM WHALE

It's hard to imagine that **SPERM WHALES**, would have a nasty trick up their sleeve, but they do. If they are threatened by killer whales, they can release a reddish-brown liquid which is derived from watery stool (or poo). The liquid clouds the water, helping them to escape their attacker. Sometimes it is called a 'poo-nado'.

MINI MAMMALS

PYGMY HIPPOPOTAMUS

The hippopotamus we all know and love is a gigantic beast, up to 5 metres (16 ft) in length and weighing up to 5 tonnes (11,000 lb). Though it looks identical, the **PYGMY HIPPOPOTAMUS** has a mass of just 160–270 kg (350–600 lb), about one-twentieth the weight of its chunky cousin, and has the body length of a wolf. It's rarer too, and is confined to the forests of West Africa, mainly Liberia and some neighbouring countries.

PYGMY WHITE-TOOTHED SHREW

Only tipping the scales at about 2 g (1/14 oz), **PYGMY WHITE-TOOTHED SHREWS** weigh less than a sugar cube and are the world's smallest land mammal. They have a body length of 4 cm (1 ½ in) and prey on crickets and other insects that are the same size as they are. Being small means they have a high metabolism, and their heart rate tops 1,500 beats per minute. They are found in southern Europe, North Africa and parts of Asia.

JAVA MOUSE DEER

With a head and body length of 46 to 56 cm (18 to 22 in), the **JAVA MOUSE DEER**, or chevrotain, is the size of a European rabbit. It is the proud owner of the title of the world's smallest artiodactyl – the group of animals that includes antelopes, camels, giraffes, pigs and hippos, as well as deer. It lives on Java (and possibly Bali), in Indonesia, and, unsurprisingly given its size, it is shy and rarely seen.

PETER'S MOUSE LEMUR

Primates are the groups of animals that include lemurs, monkeys, chimpanzees and, of course, humans! They range in size from the gorilla, which can weigh up to 170 kg (374 lb), to **PETER'S MOUSE LEMUR**, which, with a head and body length of 12 cm (4 ¾ in), is not much bigger than a mouse and has a body weight of about 55 g (2 oz). This tiny, distant relative of ours is only found in western Madagascar.

COLOSSAL SQUID

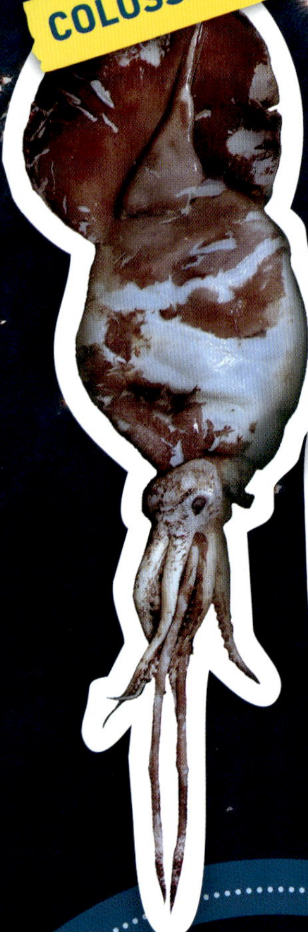

The rarely seen **COLOSSAL SQUID** is the heaviest invertebrate on the planet, weighing up to 495 kg (1,100 lb). The colossal squid does not grow as long as giant squid however, which are reported to reach 15 metres (49 ½ ft). Its eyes are bigger than footballs and help it see in the darkness of the deep sea. Like all squid, colossal squid have eight arms and two longer tentacles (up to 2.1 metres or 7 ft), and the tentacles have rows of rotating hooks that are used for grabbing and holding prey.

GIANTS OF THE

SALTWATER CROCODILE

This ferocious ocean-going crocodile can reach jaw-dropping proportions – the longest ever recorded is said to have measured 7 metres (23 ft)! Not only is it the largest reptile, but the **SALTWATER CROCODILE** also holds the record for the strongest bite of any animal. Its jaws are filled with up to 66 teeth each up to 13 cm (5 in) long, and it snaps those teeth together with such force that some scientists think it could even match the snap of the mighty *Tyrannosaurus rex*.

SEA

BLUE WHALE

This animal isn't just large, it's ginormous! It can grow to as long as 30 metres (100 ft), which makes it possibly the biggest animal ever. Pretty much everything about the **BLUE WHALE** is massive – its heart is the size of a small car, its tongue weighs as much as a male rhinoceros and it eats up to 40 million krill (tiny shrimp-like animals) a day!

WHALE SHARKS aren't whales, but the world's biggest fish! The longest reliably recorded whale shark was a whopping 18.8 metres (62 ft) from head to tail, which is longer than an articulated lorry, and their mouths can stretch to more than 1 metre (3 ⅓ ft) wide. They are filter feeders, taking large gulps of seawater containing krill and other small sea creatures that stay behind as the seawater leaves their mouths. They have about 3,000 tiny teeth in each jaw (each less than 6 mm in height) – they're not used for eating and we don't know what their purpose is.

WHALE SHARK

WHAT A SHOW-OFF!

FRILL-NECKED LIZARD

Both male and female **FRILL-NECKED LIZARDS** possess spectacular frills, which they use for communication and scaring off predators. Males also use them in displays when they are fighting with other males. This involves repeated fanning of the frill, head-bobbing, tail-lashing and waving of the forelimbs. Scientists have found males with a more intense red-orange colouration on their frill have a competitive advantage over rivals.

PEACOCK SPIDER

With brightly-coloured abdomens, male **PEACOCK SPIDERS** are the show-offs of the spider world. They are tiny, with a body length of just 0.5 cm (1/5 in) and are only found in the south of Australia. There are 59 described species (but seven new species were discovered in 2016, so there may be more), and each species has different colours and patterns. To impress females, males unfold special parts of their abdomens in a way that mimics male peacock tails.

PEAFOWL

Male **PEAFOWL** – peacocks – have one of the most spectacular courtship displays of the bird world. When their train, which can be up to 1.6 metres (5 ¼ ft) long, is lifted vertically, it reveals dozens of eye-like markings known as ocelli. The longer and brighter the display, the more attractive the male. Scientists theorize that if he can put this much energy into growing feathers that are otherwise completely useless and indeed an additional burden, it is a sign to females that he must have really good genes.

RIBBON-TAILED ASTRAPIA

The peacock might (arguably) take the overall accolade for showiest display, but the male **RIBBON-TAILED ASTRAPIA** wins the prize for the most outrageous tail feathers – they are up to 90 cm (3 ft) long, more than three times the length of the astrapia's body! This is a bird of paradise from New Guinea and, during its courtship display, the tail feathers are held up and arched to impress the female.

HONEYBEE

By living together in colonies of up to 60,000 individuals, **HONEYBEES** can carry out tasks such as complex nest construction, communication and defence that other insects are unable to. In any hive, there are three kinds of bees – the queen, who lays eggs and controls the hive with chemicals called pheromones; male drones, whose only job is to mate with the queen; and female workers who take on all the practical tasks within the hive.

AFRICAN WILD DOG

AFRICAN WILD DOGS can hunt together in packs of up to 40 animals (though more usually 7 to 15). They pursue prey much bigger than themselves such as wildebeest, but still achieve an impressive 80 per cent success rate in catching their prey – lions only manage 30 per cent – because they work so well together. They cooperate in caring for pups, as well as for sick or wounded members of the pack, with the whole group controlled by an alpha pair.

LION

LIONS are unique among the cat family in that they live highly social lives in large groups known as prides, though they work together much less than canids such as wolves. In Etosha, Namibia, lions specialize in hunting springboks, which they can only catch by working together. In Tanzania's Serengeti, lions hunting together is less common, but in any pride, females share the duties of looking after and feeding offspring.

WORKING TOGETHER

MEERKATS, which are members of the mongoose family, live in southern Africa in large groups of up to 30 or even 50 individuals. They have complex, social lives and take it in turns, for example, to act as sentinels, looking out for predators during the day. But there is a darker side to their cooperation – dominant pairs rule the roost and don't allow junior females to reproduce. If they do, the alpha females will kill the unwanted pups.

MEERKAT

THE TOOL USERS

CHIMPANZEES use tools for very different tasks – they use sticks to 'fish' for ants and termites, stones to crack nuts and they chew up leaves to use as a sponge to absorb water. There is a strong cultural element to their tool use – chimps in different parts of Africa have different traditions. Chimps are rare among animals in adapting what they find to make it more useful – stripping leaves from a twig so that they can poke it into a termite hole, for example.

SEA OTTER

SEA OTTERS feed by putting a stone on their chest when floating on their backs in the sea and then taking a mussel, crab or sea urchin and pounding it against the stone to crack it open. In a paper published in 1964, researchers observed how it took between 6 and 88 blows before they could feed. After they've eaten, they dive down in search of more food, often holding the stone under their armpit.

BOTTLENOSE DOLPHIN

BOTTLENOSE DOLPHINS in Shark Bay on the west coast of Australia pick up sponges from the seabed and fit them onto their beaks, just like a glove for a nose. The sponges protect the dolphins' sensitive skin as they poke around on the ocean floor for food, and they may even use them to stir up the sand to flush out prey. Most 'spongers' are female, and the practice is passed down from mothers to daughters.

Like sea otters, **EGYPTIAN VULTURES** also use stones to crack open shells – in their case, it's the shells of ostrich eggs which, at roughly 20 times the size of a chicken's egg, make a large and tasty meal. In Israel, ravens have been observed working in pairs to take advantage of the vultures' work, driving them away before they can eat their fill.

EGYPTIAN VULTURE

BARN OWL

A **BARN OWL'S** hearing has been shown to be 10 times more sensitive than a human's. But its real super-power is its ability to detect subtle differences between what it's hearing with its left and right ears, which are not located precisely symmetrically. That allows it to work out exactly the direction from which the noises and movements of a mouse or vole are coming from, enabling it to strike with deadly accuracy.

GREATER WAX MOTH

The animal that can hear the highest frequency sounds in the world isn't a bat or a dolphin, it's the **GREATER WAX MOTH.** It can hear anything up to 300 kHz, nearly double that of dolphins, so it can hear sounds of calls made by bats that want to eat it. It's a great example of what's called the 'evolutionary arms race', where animals develop more extreme systems (in this case hearing) in response to the threats they face.

ELEPHANT

Scientists believe **ELEPHANTS** can detect rainfall from a distance of 280 km (175 miles), and that it's either the sound of rain drumming on the ground or that of thunder that they are picking up. Elephants use very low sounds to communicate over long distances, and it's this ability that probably enables them to hear rain from so far away. Studies have shown they will move towards the rain, as it offers the promise of fresh water and new growth.

ACUTE HEARING

BAT

BATS use echolocation to hunt and navigate. They produce pulses, in the range of 20 to 150 kHz (that humans cannot usually hear – we don't hear above 20 kHz). These pulses hit objects and bounce back, giving the bats information on the distance, direction of travel and speed, size, shape and even texture of the object. They gradually increase the pulse rate as they close in on a target (usually an insect) until they may be giving out up to 200 pulses a second.

NOSES WITH

SAIGA ANTELOPES, which are found in open, grassy plains of Central Asia, have an unusual, humped, hanging nose with large nostrils that point downwards. These super snouts have mucous glands and hairs that filter dust kicked up by the herd during the summer, and they warm icy, cold air before it reaches the lungs during the winter. Saigas are an ancient species that once lived alongside sabre-toothed cats and woolly mammoths.

STAR-NOSED MOLE

The snout on this mammal is quite extraordinary! Not only can the 22 wiggling tentacles detect prey moving underground, which helps when you're almost blind and it's pitch black, but the **STAR-NOSED MOLE** has also developed a way to smell underwater. It blows out air bubbles and then sucks them back in, detecting the scent of any aquatic insects on the bubble. It's an excellent swimmer and can stay underwater for up to 30 seconds while tracking down its next meal.

A DIFFERENCE

LANTERN FLY

It might look like a superlong nose, but the **LANTERN FLY'S** snout is really an extended mouth – it's hollow and the insect uses it like a straw to suck out sweet-tasting sap from tree bark. Seen from head-on the fly looks a bit like a rhino. It was once thought that their long snouts glowed in the dark – hence the name. There are hundreds of different species, mainly found in the world's tropical regions.

TAPIR

The **TAPIR'S** flexible nose isn't just for show, or to smell things with – which it does very well – it's super handy too. The tapir can move it in all directions and uses it to pick fruits and strip leaves from trees, like an elephant uses it trunk. And when the tapir is underwater, it can even poke its nose above the water's surface and use it as a snorkel! There are five species, four of them native to Central and South America and one to Asia.

STONEFISH

It's clear to see how the STONEFISH got its name – a master of camouflage it can quite easily change itself to look like a stone. Combine that with the fact that it's also the world's most venomous known fish – just one sting can be fatal to humans – and you've got yourself one scary sea creature! In fact, its spines are so sharp they've been known to pierce thick-soled boots.

SEAHORSE

SEAHORSES can't outswim their predators so instead they disappear! They can change the colour of their bumpy spiny skin to match the coral or sea plants that they're hiding in. Being super difficult to spot also helps seahorses ambush their prey. They wait, hidden, for a meal to pass by then suck it up through their tube-like mouth before swallowing it whole! And not only that, a seahorse can move its eyes in opposite directions – one looks for food and the other watches out for predators.

SAHARAN SAND VIPER

With scales that look like grains of sand, this small but scary snake wiggles its body from side to side to bury itself in its desert home. With just its eyes peeking out, the SAHARAN SAND VIPER stays frozen in place, nearly impossible to see, waiting to ambush any unsuspecting lizard or gecko that passes by.

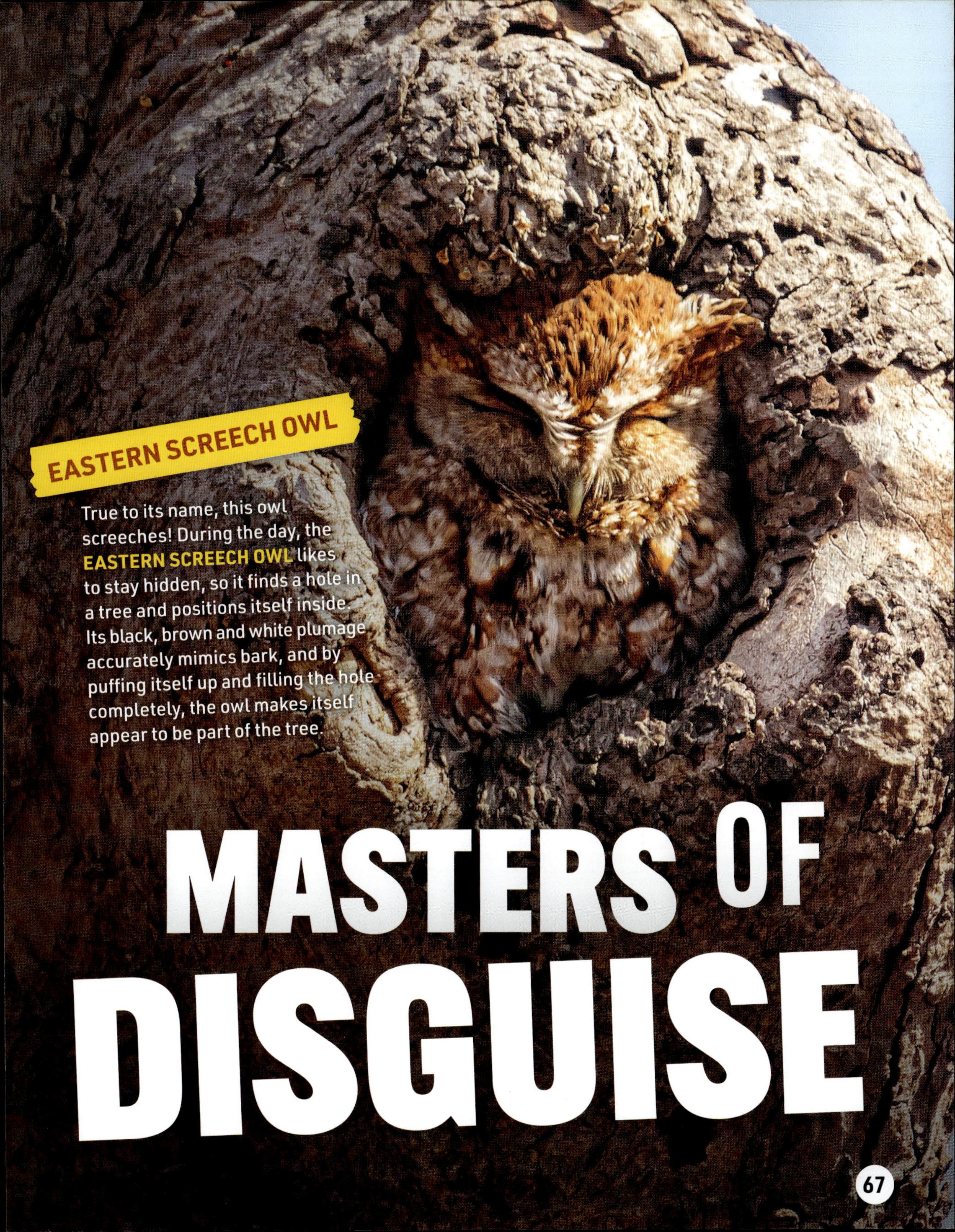

EASTERN SCREECH OWL

True to its name, this owl screeches! During the day, the **EASTERN SCREECH OWL** likes to stay hidden, so it finds a hole in a tree and positions itself inside. Its black, brown and white plumage accurately mimics bark, and by puffing itself up and filling the hole completely, the owl makes itself appear to be part of the tree.

MASTERS OF DISGUISE

WALRUS

It's not only elephants that have tusks. **WALRUSES** – one of the largest members of the family that includes seals and sealions – have tusks that can grow 1 metre (40 in) long and, like elephants, these are actually greatly elongated teeth growing out of the upper jaw. The tusks are used by males to fight each other for dominance over a group of females, as protection against predators and to help haul themselves onto ice floes where they rest.

NARWHAL

With their single spiralled tusks that can grow to 3 metres (120 in) long, **NARWHALS** are surely the planet's most distinctive cetaceans. They actually possess only two teeth, and sometimes both develop into these gnarly spears – although this is very rare. Narwhals live in the Arctic, where they feed on fish, squid and prawns. Though narwhals have been seen wielding their tusks to hit and stun fish, it is mainly males that have them so they are probably used to establish sexual dominance, in the same way deer use their antlers.

CHINESE WATER DEER

Unlike almost all other deer, **CHINESE WATER DEER** have no antlers, but males do possess quite substantial downward pointing canine teeth that can be 5 cm (2 in) long. They use them for fighting during the breeding season. Native to the Yangtze flood plain of eastern China and Korea, the species is rare, though there is a relatively healthy population in parts of the UK following accidental releases in the middle of the 20th century.

ARMED TO THE TEETH

HERCULES BEETLE

Though the bodies of **HERCULES BEETLES** are not especially large, they are nevertheless the world's longest beetles because of their huge, protruding upper horn. With the horn, males can be up to 19 cm (7 ½ in) long, making them the same length as a wood mouse! Found in South and Central America and the Caribbean, males use their horns for fighting, with one winning by lifting its opponent up and slamming him down again, like a professional wrestler.

NATURE'S MIMICS

AFRICAN GREY PARROT

Like many parrots, and indeed some other birds, **AFRICAN GREY PARROTS** are brilliant mimics, but they are so much more than that too. They are the equal of young children in their understanding of numbers, and they have preferences for different types of music and can sing along too. One African grey called Max almost became involved in a court case when its owner was murdered – the parrot was heard repeating 'Richard, no, no, no!' after the killing.

Parrots can sing along with music

LYGODIUM SPIDER MOTH

The **LYGODIUM SPIDER MOTH** is a double mimic – as an adult, patterns on its wings look like spindly orange legs, making it resemble members of the crab spider family, probably to act as a defence against spider predation. Its caterpillars are also masters of disguise and have evolved to look like some beetle larvae. The species was discovered in Thailand in 2005.

DECORATOR CRAB

The **DECORATOR CRAB** could have been called the dressing-up crab, because it covers itself with pieces of seaweed, coral, rocks or even small animals, attaching them to hooked bristles on the back of its shell. The adornments are sometimes described as being like a prom dress, though they're for camouflage not for show. Some of the seaweeds, sponges and polychaetes (segmented worms) they use give off chemical defences that may be toxic or distasteful to fish that try to eat them.

LADYBIRD SPIDER

Found in North and Central Europe, **LADYBIRD SPIDERS** are brilliant mimics of – yes – ladybirds. Only the males, which are about 9 mm long (⅓ in) and about half the size of the females, get the striking red and black markings. It's thought the markings act as a fake warning to potential predators that the spiders are unpleasant to eat – because real ladybirds are. Females spend their lives in underground burrows, so they don't need the same defence.

KOALA

Living off low-nutrition eucalyptus leaves doesn't leave **KOALAS** with a lot of energy for doing much else – apart from sleeping, which they do for an estimated 18 hours a day! Their young, known as joeys, have an even stranger diet. Before they can tolerate the toxic eucalyptus, their mothers feed them a soft, runny form of their droppings called pap. Endemic to Australia, they are only found in the east and south of the country.

AMERICAN BLACK BEAR

Four out of eight species of bear hibernate (black, brown, polar and Asiatic black), and the length of that hibernation differs depending on where they are in the world. In general, the further north and the colder the winter, the longer they sleep for. **AMERICAN BLACK BEARS**, which range from Canada to Mexico, have been recorded sleeping for up to 7 ½ months a year, while brown bears typically sleep for between 5 and 7 months.

ROACH'S MOUSE-TAILED DORMOUSE

All dormice have a reputation for being sleepy, but the **ROACH'S MOUSE-TAILED DORMOUSE** has astonished scientists by appearing to doze away in hibernation for up to 8 months of the year, even during periods of relatively warm weather. It's only active between May and August. The species lives in southern Europe, with Bulgaria, Turkey and possibly Greece the only countries where it is found.

SLEEPY HEADS

THREE-TOED SLOTH

Sloths are both sleepy and slow. **THREE-TOED SLOTHS** have been found to sleep for nearly 17 hours a day, while they have a maximum speed (on the ground) of about 2.4 metres a minute, equivalent to just 0.144 km/h (0.09 mph). Put another way, while the fastest human can manage a 100 metre race in under 10 seconds, three-toed sloths, which are native to Central and South America, would take about 50 minutes to travel the same distance.

WHAT DO YOU LOOK LIKE!

AXOLOTL

In the legends of the Aztecs, **AXOLOTLS** were gods that had disguised themselves as salamanders to avoid being sacrificed. Today, we know there is an equally strange truth about these amphibians – they are neotenous, which means they remain in their larval stage throughout their lives. Only found in the lakes that used to surround Mexico City, axolotls also have remarkable healing powers. They are able to grow new limbs in just a few weeks.

STALK-EYED FLY

Though they look like antlers, those bizarre projections have eyes on the end of them. That said, male **STALK-EYED FLIES** use them in the same way a stag might use its antlers – to compete for females. In some species in this family, the eye span is greater than their body length. They don't have these eyes when they are born but, as they emerge as an adult, they swallow air through their mouths and pump this through their eye stalks to inflate them.

GLASS FROG

From above, they look like normal tree frogs, but from below **GLASS FROGS** reveal a surprising secret – they are transparent, so their bones, internal organs and muscles are all visible. Found throughout South and Central America, the frogs' transparency is believed to be a form of camouflage, making them harder to see when viewed from below.

MEXICAN MOLE LIZARD

Is it a worm? Is it a snake? Neither, it's the **MEXICAN MOLE LIZARD**, one of just three reptiles in the Bipedidae family that is remarkable for having only two legs. They have a long, pink body (which makes them resemble a worm) and a tiny pink head. The short powerful legs at the front of the body are used for digging. They are only found in the deserts of Baja California, in western Mexico, where they build intricate burrow systems.

COCONUT CRAB

Weighing up to 4 kg (9 lb) and with a leg span of more than 1 metre (3 ⅓ ft), **COCONUT CRABS** are the world's largest terrestrial invertebrates – and excellent tree climbers when the mood takes them. They have a wide-ranging diet, that includes – you guessed it – coconuts, as well as other fruits, nuts, vegetation and carrion, while also occasionally hunting and catching small mammals and birds. They usually scale trees, however, to escape from predators hunting them.

KINKAJOU

One of only two carnivores that has a prehensile tail, the **KINKAJOU** is as comfortable living in the tree canopy as any monkey. They use their tails for balance or to wrap around branches while feeding on fruit or nectar from flowers – despite being a carnivore with a carnivore's teeth, they only occasionally eat meat or eggs. Sometimes they hang from only their tail or wrap it around themselves to keep warm at night.

GREY FOX

Members of the dog family, such as wolves or Australian dingos, are not normally enthusiastic or skilful tree climbers, but there is one exception – the **GREY FOX** of North and Central America. Helped by hooked claws and specially rotating wrist joints, grey foxes scale trees such as elders and juniper in search of fruits, or to escape from danger, such as from coyotes. They might even keep their cubs up in trees to keep them safe.

CLIMBING THE HEIGHTS

SPIDER MONKEY

SPIDER MONKEYS have almost impossibly long arms which have evolved to help them move through the forest canopy in the Central and South America's rainforests where they live. Like gibbons, they use one arm after another to swing from branch to branch. Spider monkeys have other tools that gibbons don't – a prehensile tail that acts as a fifth limb and hook-like hands with elongated fingers.

THE ULTIMATE SURVIVORS

ARMADILLO LIZARD

Just like actual armadillos, **ARMADILLO LIZARDS** roll up into a ball when threatened, gripping their tail in their jaws so that they are protected by the hard bony scales on their neck, body and tail. They only live in the semi-desert Karoo region of South Africa and grow to a maximum of about 20 cm (8 in) long, including the tail. Their jaws are extremely powerful and are capable of severing the limbs of small mammals and reptiles, but they choose to feed on invertebrates such as insects – termites especially – and spiders.

WOOD FROG

WOOD FROGS are freaks of nature – they can literally survive being frozen alive. In the dead of winter in Alaska, Canada and the northern USA where they are found, 60 per cent of their body fluid freezes up, their heart stops and they stop breathing. They achieve this by producing large quantities of glucose that protects their vital organs from freezing. When spring comes, they regain consciousness within 24 hours of thawing out.

WOMBAT

WOMBATS can survive on relatively small quantities of food compared to other marsupials their size. Food takes an average of two days to pass through their gut, and during this time they extract maximum nutrition from the poor quality food they eat. Bacteria in the colon area of the gut help break down the plant material by fermenting it. Wombats are also remarkable for being able to make cube-shaped dung – but that doesn't directly help their survival!

NAKED MOLE-RAT

NAKED MOLE-RATS may look like a cloning experiment gone wrong, but they have something all of us would probably like – immunity to cancer – and they can live for up to 30 years. If humans lived as long, relative to their body size, we'd reach 600 years old. They also possess a substance called hyaluronan, which acts as a lubricant and helps them to squeeze through the underground tunnels where they live. It is thought that it is the hyaluronan that also protects them against cancer.

SEA LAMPREY

There are many animal species that have gruesome methods of devouring their prey, though the way **SEA LAMPREYS** feed on their victims is especially grisly. They possess a disc-shaped mouth ringed with sharp teeth and they use it to attach themselves to living fish. They then rasp away with a rough tongue to feed on their hosts' blood. Found in the Atlantic Ocean, they are primitive fish, lacking scales and fins, and their skeletons are made of cartilage.

TARANTULA HAWK WASP

Like aliens from a sci-fi horror film, **TARANTULA HAWK WASPS** have evolved a dark and deadly method of reproduction. Female wasps paralyse tarantulas with their venom, drag them to their burrows and lay a single egg on the spider's body. The larva burrows inside the spider's body and eats the living tarantula until emerging as an adult itself. They grow to 11 cm (4 ⅓ in) long and are found in Central and South America.

VELVET WORM

VELVET WORMS are a group of some 200 known invertebrate species that live in the tropics and cooler parts of the southern hemisphere such as New Zealand. They hunt insects, woodlice and spiders by squirting out a jet of slime that entangles and immobilizes their prey. The slime can also be used to deter their predators. They can grow to a maximum length of 20 cm (8 in) and have up to 43 pairs of stubby legs called lobopods.

EATING WITH STYLE

AYE-AYE

There's little that's normal about Madagascar's **AYE-AYE**. It's a species of lemur that has a very long middle finger, which it uses in a most unusual way. It taps tree trunks and branches and then listens with its outsize ears for any sounds of grubs – a form of echolocation. If it hears something, it gnaws its way in, using its middle finger to scoop out the prize.

HOW DO YOU DO THAT!

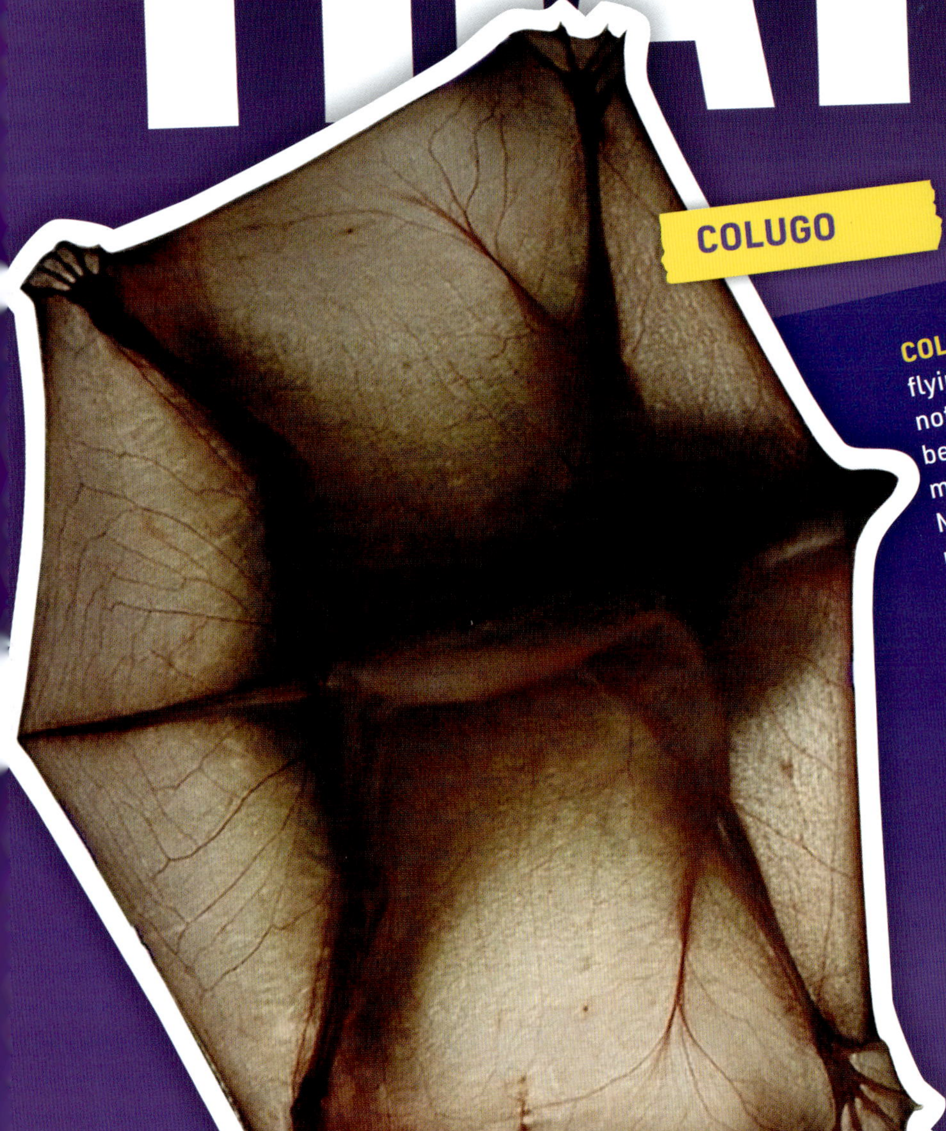

COLUGO

COLUGOS, sometimes called flying lemurs though they are not closely related, have the best gliding abilities of any mammal. Studies have shown Malayan colugos can glide for up to 15 seconds at a speed of 10 metres (11 yards) per second, covering a maximum of 150 metres (165 yards) – that is equivalent to more than 1.5 times the length of a soccer pitch. There are two colugo species, and they are both found in rainforests across Southeast Asia.

ARCHER FISH

ARCHER FISH have the unique ability to turn themselves into water pistols. By covering a groove in the roof of their mouth with their tongue they create a tube, through which they force water out at high speed at their insect prey. The prey may be standing on a branch 1.5 metres (5 ft) above them, or even moving – the force of the jet of water knocks the prey off and into the water.

There's nothing cool about getting sunburnt, and with their hairless bodies and living – as they do – under tropical African skies, **HIPPOPOTAMUSES** could easily suffer serious skin damage from exposure to the sun. To prevent this, they produce a thick clear liquid that turns red-brown. It both cools them down and acts as a sunscreen and an antibiotic. For years, it was wrongly believed hippos sweated blood – now we know they're really responsible sunbathers.

HIPPOPOTAMUS

SECRETARY BIRD

Snakes are normally the animals that others fear and avoid, but the **SECRETARY BIRDS** of sub-Saharan Africa specialize in hunting them. They attack and kill their prey by stamping on them with a force equivalent to five times their body weight and with a contact time of 0.015 seconds, which is 100 times faster than snakes can strike. They can kill cobras and black mambas, both highly venomous species.

GOLDEN-RUMPED ELEPHANT SHREW

The title for the fastest small land mammal belongs to the **GOLDEN-RUMPED ELEPHANT SHREW**. Found only in Africa, this little creature can sprint at least 25 km/h (15 mph), and, from its head to its tail is only 56 cm (20 in) long! It gets its name from its trunk-like nose and, amazingly, they are more closely related to elephants than shrews.

PEREGRINE FALCON

The **PEREGRINE FALCON** is the fastest animal of any kind. When diving from great heights to catch birds in mid-air, or during territorial displays, it can reach a speed of at least 200 km/h (124 mph) and probably as much as 250 km/h (155 mph), with the highest-ever recorded velocity of 387 km/h (242 mph). A specially adapted respiratory system allows it to carry on breathing while maintaining these speeds.

BLACK MAMBA

In short bursts a **BLACK MAMBA** can slither at up to 19 km/h (12 mph), making it the fastest snake on land. From above, its head is the shape of a coffin and though its skin is actually grey, its mouth is completely black and its potent venom can kill a human in 20 minutes.

SMALL BUT SPEEDY

GENTOO PENGUIN

The **GENTOO PENGUIN** is probably the fastest bird underwater and has been recorded swimming at speeds of about 36 km/h (22 mph). Like all penguins, gentoos appear clumsy on land, but in the sea they look like they are flying through the water, using their paddle-shaped flippers like wings. To keep their body shape compact in the water, they tuck their heads into their shoulders and press their feet to their tail, which they use to help steer.

GIANTS OF THE SKY

GIRAFFES have the world's longest necks, but their bodies are pretty tall too. From hoof to horn they can reach heights of 5 ½ metres (18 ft) – that's tall enough to peer into a first floor window! Their height, along with their excellent eyesight, helps them keep an eye out for hungry predators such as lions and hyenas. They can also hear noises that humans can't detect. To see who is stronger, males fight by bumping, ramming and pushing their long necks and heads into their opponent.

Giraffes have the same number of neck bones as us – 7!

FLYING FOX

There is a group of bats much larger than the little ones you might see flying around chasing insects. These huge bats are called **FLYING FOXES**, or fruit bats, and some of them are real monsters. The flying foxes, so called because of their dog-like faces, of Southeast Asia are one of the largest. They have a wingspan of up to 1.5 metres (5 ft), weigh more than 1 kg (2.2 lb) and have been recorded roosting together in groups of 21,000 individuals. Straw-coloured fruit bats, about half this size, congregate in a group numbering as much as 8 million. Luckily for us, they eat mainly fruit, nectar and flowers.

QUEEN ALEXANDRA'S BIRDWING BUTTERFLY

The rare **QUEEN ALEXANDRA'S BIRDWING BUTTERFLY** is the world's largest butterfly. The body of a full-grown female butterfly can reach nearly 8 cm (3 in) long, with a wingspan of up to 30 cm (1 ft). It can weigh as much as 12 g (½ oz), which is heavy for a butterfly and about the size of a small bird! They are only found in a few locations in Papua New Guinea.

WANDERING ALBATROSS

With an out-stretched wingspan of 3.5 metres (11 ½ ft) the **WANDERING ALBATROSS** can easily glide through the air for days and weeks non-stop. One bird was recorded flying right around Antarctica in 46 days. They powernap mid-air or on the surface of water, only visiting land to breed. But landing doesn't come naturally to one of the world's largest ocean birds, and they often make clumsy crash landings, sometimes tumbling over as they hit the ground!

MOSQUITO

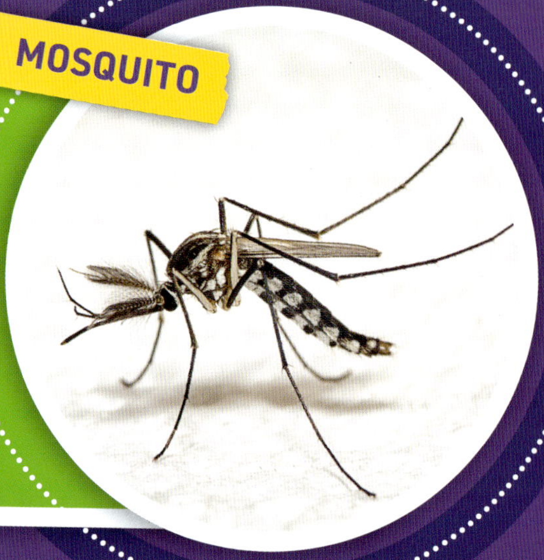

MOSQUITOES, or rather three species of mosquito, are the world's deadliest animals. They carry some of the world's worst diseases such as malaria and yellow fever, which kill hundreds of thousands of people every year. Only female mosquitoes bite – they can land on your arm and bite you without you even noticing, until the itching starts. Mosquitoes beat their wings about 1,000 times per second which creates their tell-tale buzzing sound. And this, together with their small size, means you are likely to hear one before you see it.

GOLDEN POISON-ARROW FROG

You have been warned! The **GOLDEN POISON-ARROW FROG** has a poison in its skin so potent it could kill 22,000 mice or 10 men – scientists need to wear thick gloves when handling them. It is one of many animals that sports a brightly coloured body to warn other animals to stay away. The frog only has two known enemies – the frog-eating snake, which has some immunity to its toxin and can eat juvenile frogs with no ill effects, and the indigenous people of South America who have been using its poison on the tips of their blow darts for centuries.

BRAZILIAN WANDERING SPIDER

Spiders give people the creeps and you'd be right to be scared of the **BRAZILIAN WANDERING SPIDER**! They have the most toxic venom of any spider and are very aggressive. Luckily, an antivenom is available and human deaths are now rare. They are fast moving, have large, hairy bodies and strong legs which can grow to a span of 13 to 15 cm (5 to 6 in), eight eyes, two much larger than the rest, and bright red jaws which they flash when angry.

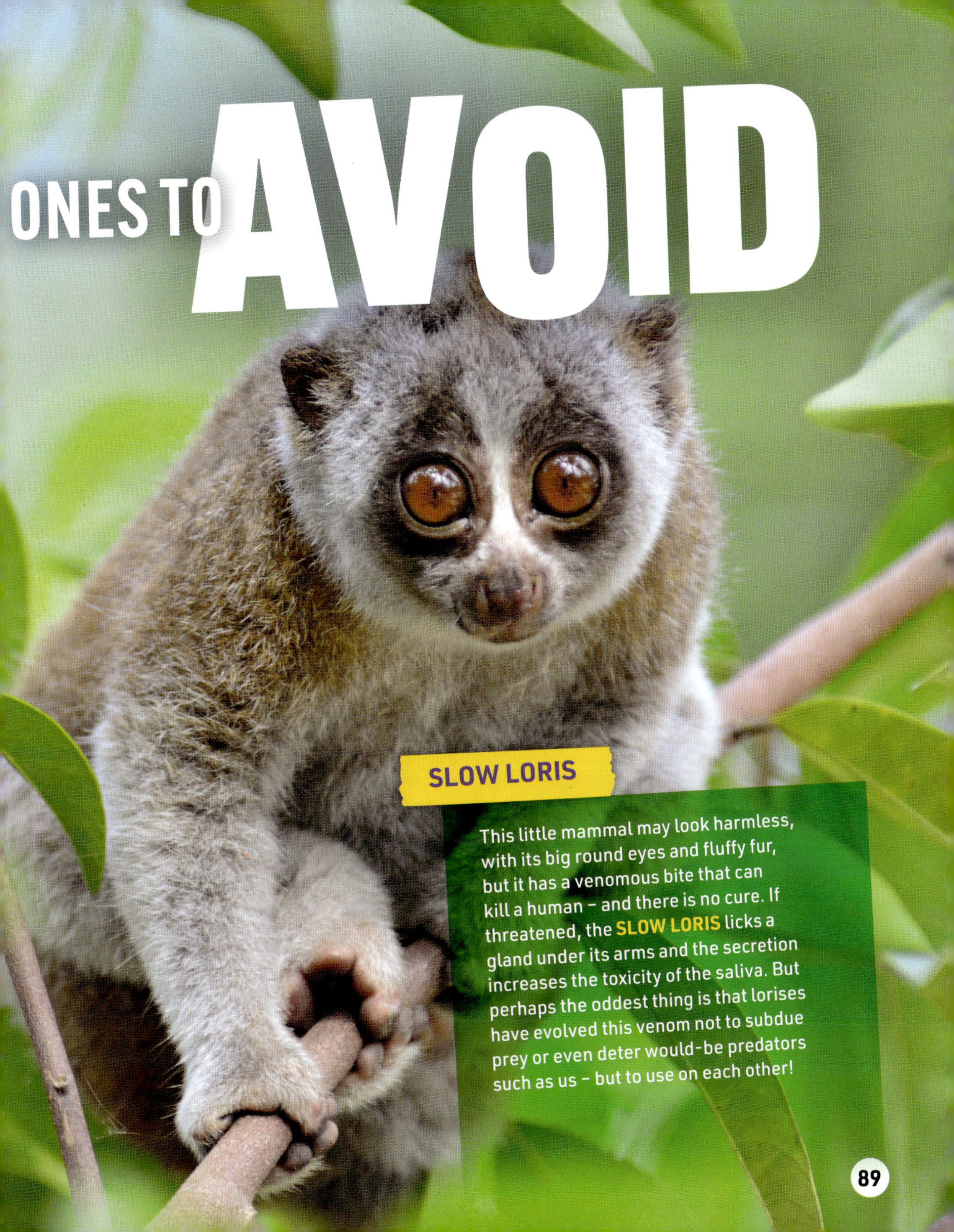

ONES TO AVOID

SLOW LORIS

This little mammal may look harmless, with its big round eyes and fluffy fur, but it has a venomous bite that can kill a human – and there is no cure. If threatened, the **SLOW LORIS** licks a gland under its arms and the secretion increases the toxicity of the saliva. But perhaps the oddest thing is that lorises have evolved this venom not to subdue prey or even deter would-be predators such as us – but to use on each other!

READY FOR ANYTHING

They're not monsters, but **GILA MONSTERS** do have a fairly monstrous last-gasp survival technique. One of very few venomous lizards in the world, they latch onto any attacker with a tenacious bite. Chewing down on the victim's flesh, venom flows along teeth in their lower jaw into the wound. Gila monsters feed on small mammals and birds, but their venom is purely for defence and is not needed to subdue their prey.

GILA MONSTER

MAD HATTERPILLAR

The caterpillar of the moth *Uraba lugens* , which is native to Australia, has the most inventive of defence mechanisms. It moults up to 13 times during its larval stage and, after every moult, it retains the hard shell that enclosed its head, building them up like hats perched on top of each other. It thrashes this strange headgear around to distract predators. Because of this behaviour the species has earned the nickname **MAD HATTERPILLAR**!

TURKEY VULTURE

Babies are renowned for the occasional projectile vomit, but **TURKEY VULTURES** take this to a new level. They can send a stream of regurgitated food 3 metres (10 ft) into the air as a defensive mechanism, and this puke is so acidic it forces potential predators to back off. Like other vultures, they also defecate on their feet, which not only kills off bacteria but keeps them cool in hot weather – a practice known as urohydrosis.

SPINY NEWT

You'd better beware if you want to eat, or even handle, a **SPINY NEWT**. It possesses an evolutionary adaptation that appears to come straight out of a sci-fi horror film, with sharp, pointed ribs poking out against its rib cage through warts in the skin. If they try to take a bite, predators receive a painful injection in the mouth. There are two species, one only found on five small Japanese islands, the other in eastern China.

SMALLEST FROG

With a body length of 7 to 8 mm (¼ to 3/10 in), the **SMALLEST FROG** has no common name and its Latin one is *Paedophryne amauensis*. Shorter than a drawing pin, it is the world's smallest known vertebrate and is more than 3,000 times smaller than the largest – the blue whale. Only discovered in New Guinea in 2009, like other similarly miniature frogs it inhabits moist leaf litter in order to minimize water loss. Until its discovery, the world's smallest vertebrate was a fish measuring 7.9 mm (3/10 in).

KITTI'S HOG-NOSED BAT

With a head and body length of 3 cm (1 in), **KITTI'S HOG-NOSED BAT** is about the size of a bumblebee. It does have a much larger wingspan (still only 15 cm/6 in), but it's comfortably the world's smallest mammal. The species is found in Thailand and Myanmar, where it roosts in limestone caves – and there are only 43 caves where it is known to live.

BARBADOS THREADSNAKE

Shorter than a standard smart phone, the **BARBADOS THREADSNAKE** is the world's smallest snake. It's 10 cm (4 in) long, as slender as a noodle and can curl up on a US quarter (25 cent coin). Females lay a single egg that hatches an offspring half the size of the adult. Thread snakes eat termites, and it's believed if the young were any smaller, there would be nothing sufficiently miniature for them to eat.

SMALLEST OF THEIR KIND

The world's smallest reptile is the **NANO CHAMELEON** of Madagascar, an animal so tiny that males measure just 2.16 cm (9/10 in) from their heads to their tails and you could fit two (one behind the other) inside a matchbox. Scientists are constantly making new discoveries in this field, with the nano chameleon taking over the 'world's smallest' title from the nosy hara leaf chameleon which took over the title from the Madagascan dwarf chameleon. What they'll call the next one is anybody's guess!

NANO CHAMELEON

INDEX

PICTURE CREDITS

p.4 ©Stu Porter/Shutterstock; p.5 top ©Photon-Photos/istock; middle ©slowmotiongli/istock; bottom ©Tom Reichner/istock; p.6 top ©Vladimir Wrangel/Shutterstock; bottom ©Nynke van Holten/Shutterstock; p.7 top ©Daniel Heuclin/naturepl.com; bottom ©oversnap/iStock; p.8 ©Professor Roy Caldwell; p.9 top ©Wang LiQiang/Shutterstock; middle ©Nuytsia@Tas/Flickr; bottom ©Nicholas Smythe/Science Photo Library; p.10 ©PHOTOOBJECT/Shutterstock; p.11 top left ©Jukka Jantunen/Shutterstock; top right ©asawinimages/Shutterstock; p.11 bottom ©fendercapture/Shutterstock; p.12 ©S.Rohrlach/iStock; p.13 top ©Simagart/Shutterstock; middle ©DiveSpin.Com/Shutterstock; bottom ©Mark Moffett/Minden/naturepl.com; p.14 top ©Rosa Jay/Shutterstock; middle ©DerrenMeadwell/iStock; bottom ©Sylvain Cordier/naturepl.com; p.15 ©Berendje Fotografie/Shutterstock; p.16 ©zaidi Razak/Shutterstock; p.17 top ©Roberto Dani/Shutterstock; middle ©Mark Bowler/naturepl.com; bottom ©Ken Griffiths/Shutterstock; p.18 top ©Francois Savigny/naturepl.com; bottom ©KUSHELEV IVAN/Shutterstock; p.19 top ©Hawaiian/iStock; bottom ©wrangel/iStock; p.20 ©ranplett/iStock; p.21 top ©Luiz Claudio Marigo/naturepl.com; middle ©CezaryKorkosz/Shutterstock; bottom ©SIMON SHIM/Shutterstock; p.22 ©Trevor Charles Graham/Shutterstock; p.23 top ©sduben/iStock; middle ©Patrick Randall; bottom ©slowmotiongli/iStock; p.24 ©Marek R. Swadzba/Shutterstock; p.25 top ©Gerald Robert Fischer/Shutterstock; bottom ©Bildagentur Zoonar GmbH/Shutterstock; p.26 ©Mlenny/iStock; p.27 top ©DmitryND/iStock; middle ©twospeeds/Shutterstock; bottom ©Nicholas Taffs/Shutterstock; p.28 ©Gerald Corsi/iStock; p.29 top ©David Havel/Shutterstock; middle ©filipfoto/iStock; bottom ©mamarama/iStock; p.30 top ©Roland Seitre/naturepl.com; middle ©4FR/iStock; bottom ©AndreAnita/iStock; p.31 ©Ava-Leigh/iStock; p.32 ©Mariko Yuki/Shutterstock; p.33 top ©Pedro Luna/Shutterstock; middle ©Alexis Fioramonti/iStock; bottom ©JNevitt/iStock; p.34 ©Vincent Pro Photo/Shutterstock; p.35 top ©Klein & Hubert/naturepl.com; middle ©Merlintuttle.org/Science Photo Library; bottom ©Vinnie Lauritsen/Shutterstock; p.36 ©Marc Lechanteur/Shutterstock; p.37 top ©esdeem/Shutterstock; middle ©Svoboda Pavel/Shutterstock; bottom ©Yatra/Shutterstock; p.38 top ©Gary E Swanson/Shutterstock; bottom ©Aleksa Georg/Shutterstock; p.39 top ©Juanmonino/iStock; bottom ©Tara Lynn and Co/Shutterstock; p.40 top ©Enrique Ascanio/Shutterstock; middle ©Tempau/iStock; bottom ©mark higgins/Shutterstock; p.41 ©HillebrandBreuker/Shutterstock; p.42 top ©Sebastian Janicki/Shutterstock; middle ©Eric Isselee/Shutterstock; bottom ©serkan mutan/Shutterstock; p.43 ©PetlinDmitry/iStock; p.44 ©bimserd/Shutterstock; p.45 top ©Agnieszka Bacal/Shutterstock; middle ©SongayeNovell/iStock; bottom ©webguzs/iStock; p.46 ©ARTYuSTUDIO/iStock; p.47 top ©FRANKHILDEBRAND/iStock; middle ©Subaqueosshutterbug/iStock; bottom ©imv/iStock; p.48 ©Lab Photo/Shutterstock; p.49 top ©Erland Refling Nielsen; middle ©7th Son Studio/Shutterstock; bottom ©kurt_G/Shutterstock; p.50 top ©johannviloria/Shutterstock; middle ©John Cancalosi/naturepl.com; bottom ©Jouan Rius/naturepl.com; p.51 ©Franco Banfi/naturepl.com; p.52 ©GeeNamp/iStock; p.53 top ©phototrip/iStock; middle ©Polbkt/Shutterstock; bottom ©Thomas Marrent/Minden/naturepl.com; pp.54–55 top ©Chase Dekker/Shutterstock; middle ©Museum of New Zealand Te Papa Tongarewa; bottom ©Coral Brunner/Shutterstock; p.55 bottom ©Onusa Putapitak/Shutterstock; p.56 © Ken Griffiths; p.57 top ©Adam Fletcher/Biosphoto; middle ©LaMccray/Shutterstock; bottom ©Tim Laman/nature/iStock; p.58 top ©florintt/iStock; middle ©Charl Senekal/iStock; bottom ©Ryan Green/iStock; p.59 ©attanan726/iStock; p.60 ©mark higgins/Shutterstock; p.61 top ©Kirsten Wahlquist/Shutterstock; middle ©Hugh Pearson/naturepl.com; bottom ©Sander Meertins/iStock; p.62 top ©Anan Kaewkhammul/Shutterstock; middle ©D. Kucharski K. Kucharska/Shutterstock; bottom ©Susan Schmitz/Shutterstock; p.63 ©CreativeNature_nl/iStock; p.64 ©Mikhail Gnatkovskiy/Shutterstock; p.65 top ©Agnieszka Bacal/Shutterstock; middle ©Chongsiri Chaitongngam/Shutterstock; bottom ©Ondrej Prosicky/Shutterstock; p.66 top ©PRILL/Shutterstock; middle ©ifish/iStock; bottom ©reptiles4all/Shutterstock; p.67 ©Jennifer Yakey-Ault/Shutterstock; p.68 top ©tryton2011/Shutterstock; middle ©dottedhippo/iStock; bottom ©R J Endall Photographer/Shutterstock; p.69 ©GlobalP/iStock; p.70 ©Richard Susanto/Shutterstock; p.70 top ©Mark Bowler/naturepl.com; middle ©Mike Workman/Shutterstock; bottom ©aaltair/Shutterstock; p.72 left ©Manuk/Shutterstock; right ©TangoFoxtrot2018/Shutterstock; p.73 top Nedyalkov, Nedko & Popgeorgiev, Georgi & Staneva, Anna. (2018). Updated distribution of the elusive Roach's mouse-tailed dormouse, Myomimus roachi Bate, 1937 (Mammalia: Rodentia: Gliridae) in Bulgaria. Historia naturalis Bulgarica. 29. 3-8. 10.48027/hnb.29.01001; bottom ©GeorgePeters/iStock; p.74 ©Arm001/shutterstock; p.75 top ©khlungcenter/Shutterstock; middle ©Dr Morley Read/Shutterstock; bottom ©Daniel Rosenberg; p.76 top ©Tomas Kotouc/Shutterstock; middle ©Martin Pelanek/Shutterstock; bottom ©Geoffrey Kuchera/Shutterstock; p.77 ©KenCanning/iStock; p.78 ©eptiles4all/iStock; p.79 top ©Viktor Loki/Shutterstock; middle ©marco3t/iStock; bottom ©Eric Isselee/Shutterstock; p.80 top ©Gena Melendrez/Shutterstock; middle ©Tom Wurl/Shutterstock; bottom ©Brent Stephenson/naturepl.com; p.81 ©Suzi Eszterhas/Minden/naturepl.com; p.82 ©hawats/iStock; p.83 top ©Wirestock Creators//Shutterstock; middle ©Eric Baccega/naturepl.com; bottom ©THEGIFT777/iStock; p.84 top ©Marius Dobilas/Shutterstock; middle ©Harry Collins Photography/Shutterstock; bottom ©tirc83/iStock; p.85 ©burroblando/iStock; p.86 ©Rich Townsend/iStock; p.87 top ©CraigRJD/iStock; middle ©Russell Marshall/Shutterstock; bottom ©Streeteh/Shutterstock; p.88 top ©nuwatphoto/Shutterstock; middle ©kikkerdirk/iStock; bottom ©Tacio Philip Sansonovski/Shutterstock; p.89 ©Conservationist/Shutterstock; p.90 ©reptiles4all/iStock; p.91 top ©James Wood; middle ©MattCuda/iStock; bottom ©Dr Joachim Nerz; p.92 top ©Eric N. Rittmeyer et al, Ecological Guild Evolution and the Discovery of the World's Smallest Vertebrate, Plos One, January 11, 2012; middle ©Blair Hedges, Penn State; bottom ©MerlinTuttle.org/Science Photo Library; p.93 ©Frank Glaw, Jörn Köhler, Oliver Hawlitschek, Fanomezana M. Ratsoavina, Andolalao Rakotoarison, Mark D. Scherz & Miguel Vences, CC BY 4.0 <https://creativecommons.org/licenses/by/4.0>, via Wikimedia Commons

Every effort has been made to contact and accurately credit all copyright holders. If we have been unsuccessful, we apologise and welcome correction for future editions and reprints.

First published by the Natural History Museum, Cromwell Road, London SW7 5BD
Reprinted 2024

A catalogue record for this book is available from the British Library.

ISBN 978 0 56509 532 1

10 9 8 7 6 5 4 3 2

Design by **Fuszion**
Reproduction by **Saxon Digital Services**
Printed by **Toppan Leefung Ltd, China**